COLLINS GEM GUIDES

WILD FLOWERS

Marjorie Blamey

Richard Fitter

First published 1980

© Richard Fitter and Marjorie Blamey 1980

ISBN 0 00 458801 0

Colour reproduction by Adroit Photo-Litho Ltd, Birmingham

Filmset by Jolly & Barber Ltd, Rugby

Printed and bound by Wm Collins Sons and Co Ltd, Glasgow

Reprint 20 19 18 17 16 15 14 13

Contents

How to Use this Book

The enjoyment of wild flowers is a pastime which needs no equipment – just your legs. Since Britain has over 1,500 native wild flowers, this book contains only a selection, aimed at those who know little or nothing about plants, and excludes all trees and shrubs, all grasses, sedges, rushes and waterweeds, and some common weeds. Many plants are protected – remember always to *take the book to the plant*, not vice versa.

The drawing below shows the various parts of a flower, and is followed by a few useful definitions.

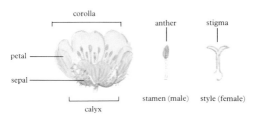

corolla

anther

stigma

petal

sepal

calyx

stamen (male)

style (female)

Anther: the tip of the stamen, producing the male pollen. **Bracts:** small, usually leaf-like organs just below the flowers. **Calyx:** the sepals as a whole, when they are joined. **Lanceolate** leaves are spear-shaped, narrowly oval and pointed. **Petals:** usually conspicuous organs above the sepals, and surrounding the reproductive parts of a flower. **Pinnate** leaves grow in pairs on either side of the stalk. **Sepals** form a ring immediately below the petals and are usually green or brown. **Stamens:** the male organs of a flower. **Stigma:** the surface at the tip of the style, which receives pollen. **Styles:** the columns of filaments leading from the female organs to the stigma.

The illustrated key, based on colour and flower shapes, will help you identify the flowers you find. All the colour plates in the book are life-size. The black-and-white drawings are smaller, to indicate the whole plant, or some detail of it.

Flowering plants are arranged in two groups: monocotyledons, which have only one seed-leaf, and dicotyledons, which have two seed-leaves. Within these major divisions the plants are grouped first into families, then into genera and finally by species. The first of the two Latin names is that of the genus, and the second that of the species.

Readers whose interest has been aroused may like to extend their knowledge with two other books: M. Blamey and R. Fitter, *Collins Handguide to the Wild Flowers of Britain and Northern Europe*; and R. Fitter, A. Fitter and M. Blamey, *The Wild Flowers of Britain and Northern Europe*.

Key

This key is broken down (1) into two main sections: 'Individual large or conspicuous flowers', starting below, and 'Small individual flowers in heads or spikes', on p. 13. Under these headings it is further divided (2) by flower shape and then (3), where appropriate, by the number of petals. Within each of these last divisions the flowers are grouped according to shape and basic colour, starting with white flowers and moving through yellow, green, pink, red and lilac/purple to blue.

Individual large or conspicuous flowers

Open, star-like or saucer-shaped flowers

Two petals

 Enchanter's Nightshade 101

 Goldilocks Buttercup 33

Three petals

 Common Water-plantain 213

 Goldilocks Buttercup 33

Common Water-Plantain 213

Four petals

 Squinancywort 131, Woodruff 132, Bedstraws 134, 135, Cleavers 135

7

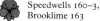

English Stonecrop 58, Purging Flax 81, Chickweed Wintergreen 123, Bogbean 125, Black Nightshade 153

 Marsh Marigold 31, St John's Worts 93, 94, Yellow Loosestrife 121, Yellow Pimpernel 121, Creeping Jenny 121

 Knotgrass 18, Corn Spurrey 23, Water Crowfoot 37, Sundews 56, Grass of Parnassus 61, Saxifrages 59, Meadowsweet 62, Dropwort 62, Strawberries 66, Wood Sorrel 81, White Rock-rose 98

 Pansies 97

 Lady's Mantles 65

 Sweet Violet 95

 White Bryony 99

 Agrimony 63, Creeping Cinquefoil 68, Silverweed 68, Primrose 119, Cowslip 119, Oxlips 120

 Sea Sandwort 20

 Red Campion 25, Sticky Catchfly 27, Cranesbills 82, Storksbills 82, Herb Robert 84

 Biting Stonecrop 60

 Buttercups 32, 33, Lesser Spearwort 33, Yellow Anemone 35, Rock-roses 98, Mulleins 155

 Red Campion 25, Maiden Pink 27

 Ragged Robin 25, Mallows 91, 92

 Bogbean 125

9

Knotgrass 18,
Soapwort 26,
Cranesbills 82,
Storksbills 82

 Sea Spurreys 23,
Common Centaury
126

 Scarlet Pimpernel
122

 Mallows 91, 92

 Marsh Cinquefoil 67,
Water Avens 67,
Bittersweet 153

 Corn Cockle 26,
Houndstongue 137,
Vervain 140

 Wood Cranesbill 83,
Gentians 127

 Violets 95, 96,
Pansies 97

 Meadow Cranesbill
83, Borage 137,
Forgetmenots 138,
Viper's Bugloss 139,
Green Alkanet 139

Six or more petals

 White Water-lily 28,
Wood Anemone 36,
Chickweed
Wintergreen 123

 Meadowsweet 62

 Ramsons 217

 Yellow Water-lily 29,
Lesser Celandine 36,
Yellow Anemone 35

 Yellow-wort 126,
Bog Asphodel 216

 Wild Mignonette 55,
Black Bryony 99

 Flowering Rush 215

 Hepatica 34

 Purple Loosestrife
105

 Spring Squill 218

Vervain 140, Self-heal 142, Ground Ivy 142, Mints 149, Basil Thyme 152, Figworts 156, Red Bartsia 159

 Butterworts 168

 Orchids 223–7

 Vetches 72, 73, Tares 73, 74

 Bugle 141

 Skullcap 141

 Milkworts 90

Miscellaneous shapes

 Globe Flower 30

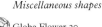 Wild Daffodil 219

 Yellow Iris 221

 Foxglove 158

 Lords and Ladies 220

 Giant Bellflower 179

Small individual flowers in heads or spikes
Tightly packed globular heads

 Clovers 80

 Sanicle 106

Stinking Chamomile 183, Michaelmas Daisy 185, Mountain Everlasting 186, Ox-eye Daisy 192

Spurges 85–7, Wild Parsnip 115, Rock Samphire 116, Alexanders 116, Ploughman's Spikenard 184, Tansy 184

 Fleabane 187, Corn Marigold 193, Coltsfoot 194, Ragworts 195, 196, Groundsel 197, Carline Thistle 198

Petty Spurge 88

 Sea Aster 185, Michaelmas Daisy 185, Knapweeds 203

Angelica 113, Hemp Agrimony 180

Field Madder 131, Cornflower 205

Scabiouses 174

Flat heads

Hoary Cress 54, Cow Parsley 108, Rough Chervil 108, Hedge Parsley 109, Wild Carrot 109, Burnet Saxifrage 110, Pignut 110, Ground Elder 111, Fool's Parsley 111, Hogweed 112, Angelica 113, Hemlock 114, Fool's Watercress 115, Yarrow 189, Sneezewort 189

Leafless spikes

 Redshank 18, Sundews 56

Haresfoot Clover 79, Hoary Plantain 169

 White Melilot 77, Thyme-leaved Speedwell 162

Leafy whorls

Mints 149

 Lady's Mantles 65, Spurges 88, Black Bryony 99

 Spurreys 23, Squinancywort 131, Marjoram 151, Valerians 171, Hemp Agrimony 180

Loose-stalked clusters

 Thyme-leaved Sandwort 20, Lesser Stitchwort 21, Mouse-ears 22, Chickweed 22, Corn Spurrey 23, Meadow-rue 37, Rue-leaved Saxifrage 59, Meadowsweet 62, Dropwort 62, Fairy Flax 81, Squinancywort 131, Woodruff 132, Bedstraws 134, 135, Cleavers 135, Red Valerian 172

 Red Valerian 172

Flowers solitary or in pairs at base of leaves

 Knotgrass 18, Cleavers 135, Solomon's Seal 216

 Solomon's Seal 216

 Golden Saxifrage 60, Lady's Bedstraw 133, Helichrysum 186, Mugwort 190, Groundsels 197,

 Knotgrass 18, Sea Milkwort 122

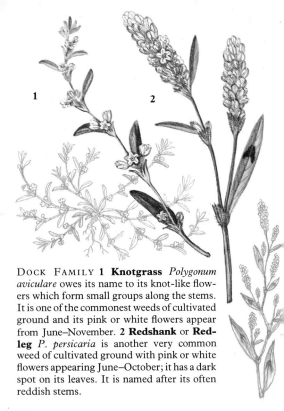

DOCK FAMILY **1 Knotgrass** *Polygonum
aviculare* owes its name to its knot-like flowers which form small groups along the stems.
It is one of the commonest weeds of cultivated
ground and its pink or white flowers appear
from June–November. **2 Redshank** or **Red-
leg** *P. persicaria* is another very common
weed of cultivated ground with pink or white
flowers appearing June–October; it has a dark
spot on its leaves. It is named after its often
reddish stems.

DOCK FAMILY **1 Common Sorrel** *Rumex acetosa* is the plant that turns meadows crimson in late May and early June; it has a distinctive acid taste that once made it a favoured salad plant. **2 Sheep's Sorrel** *R. acetosella* is, with Common Sorrel, one of the most attractive members of the dock family. It is a smaller plant and grows on poorer, sandy and usually more or less acid soils, flowering from May–August. It was evidently once regarded as a salad plant fit only for sheep.

PINK FAMILY **1 Sea Sandwort** *Honkenya peploides* is found almost exclusively on sandy seashores, and has fleshy leaves, greenish-white flowers appearing May–August, and distinctive green berry-like fruits (**1a**) as large as a small garden pea. **2 Thyme-leaved Sandwort** *Arenaria serpyllifolia* is a common weed of bare places with small white flowers appearing from April–November. It is one of the commonest of the large array of small white-flowered chickweed-like plants to which our ancestors gave the name of sand-wort, meaning plants (worts) that grow in sandy places.

PINK FAMILY Stitchworts *Stellaria* differ from chickweeds in having long strap-like leaves instead of short broad ones. **1 Greater Stitchwort** *S. holostea* has the largest flowers (about 2.5cm across) of any of the stitchworts, and is one of the commonest and most attractive wild flowers of the spring hedgerows and woodland borders throughout the British Isles. **2 Lesser Stitchwort** *S. graminea* has smaller flowers, less than half the size, and grows especially in heathy, more or less acid grassland; its flowering period lasts from May–August and it is as widespread as Greater Stitchwort.

PINK FAMILY Mouse-ears *Cerastium* used to be called mouse-eared chickweeds. Chickweeds *Stellaria* proper are so called because domestic fowls like cropping them. **1 Field Mouse-ear** *C. arvense* has large flowers, over 1cm across, appearing April–August. It grows on limy soils in dry open places. **2 Common Mouse-ear** *C. fontanum* is very common and widespread, with much smaller flowers in April–November. It grows in grassy and bare places. **3 Common Chickweed** *S. media* is one of the commonest weeds of cultivated ground and flowers throughout the year except in snow or hard frost.

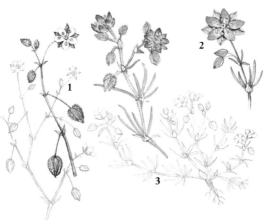

PINK FAMILY **1 Corn Spurrey** *Spergula arvensis* is a small weedy plant with narrow linear leaves. It grows in light soils, avoiding lime, often as an arable weed, and its white flowers appear from May–September. Its variety *sativa* is still sometimes grown as a catch crop on the Continent. **2 Greater Sea Spurrey** *Spergularia media* is a similar plant which grows only in saltmarshes by the sea. **3 Lesser Sea Spurrey** *S. marina* also grows in saltmarshes but can always be distinguished by its smaller flowers which measure 60–80mm across instead of 80–125mm. Both sea spurreys can be found in flower from May–September.

PINK FAMILY Campions *Silene* all have rather inflated calyces. **1 Sea Campion** *S. maritima* flowers
from April onwards, and grows on cliffs and shingle
by the sea and on some mountains. **2 Bladder
Campion** *S. vulgaris* is named after its inflated
calyx. It grows in bare and sparsely grassy places,
especially on limy soils, and its smaller flowers on
longer stems appear from May–September. **3 White
Campion** *S. alba* is taller than Bladder Campion, is
green and stickily hairy instead of greyish and hairless, and flowers from May–October. It grows in
cornfields and on waste ground.

PINK FAMILY **1 Red Campion** *Silene dioica* resembles White Campion (opposite) but has deep rose-pink flowers; plants with pale pink flowers are probably hybrids between the 2 species. It grows in hedge-banks, on the borders of woods and on grassy sea cliffs, flowering from March–November. **2 Ragged Robin** *Lychnis flos-cuculi* has flowers which look ragged because of their narrow petal segments and appear from May–August. It grows in damp and marshy grassland and fens, often with water underfoot.

PINK FAMILY **1 Soapwort** *Saponaria officinalis* contains saponin, which foams with water and was once used as a soap substitute. A widespread relic of cultivation, often in a double-flowered form, it grows on roadsides and by streams, flowering June–September. **2 Corn Cockle** *Agrostemma githago*, once an abundant cornfield weed ('cockle' means weed) is now rare because of modern herbicides. Its purple flowers appear May–August.

PINK FAMILY **1 Maiden Pink** *Dianthus deltoides* is very local in dry, grassy, usually sandy places, with white-spotted pink flowers 15–20mm across, like a small garden pink, appearing June–September. Deptford Pink *D. armeria* has clusters of smaller flowers surrounded by long green leafy bracts. **2 Sticky Catchfly** *Lychnis viscaria*, sometimes seen in gardens, has sticky hairs just below each leaf-junction and bright rose-pink flowers appearing May–August. A rare plant, it grows on rocks in about 8 places in Scotland and Wales, including King Arthur's Seat in Edinburgh.

27

WATER-LILY FAMILY **White Water-lily**
Nymphaea alba. Although this water-lily is
widely planted in ornamental waters it is less
common as a wild plant and is largely confined to lakes and lochans (small lochs) in the
north and west of the British Isles. Its leaves
are smaller than those of the Yellow Water-
lily (opposite) and more or less circular, while
the flowers, which are 50–200mm across and
appear from June–September, float on the
surface of the water. Water-lilies are, of
course, in no way related to the true lilies.

WATER-LILY FAMILY **Yellow Water-lily**
Nuphar lutea is common in rivers, where its
large oval leaves, up to 45cm across, float on
the surface; its yellow flowers, much smaller
than those of the White Water-lily (opposite),
project a few centimetres above the water
from June–September. The slightly heady
fragrance of the flowers, combined with the
flask shape of the fruits, has earned it the folk
name of Brandy Bottle. There are also some
submerged leaves which are very loose and
cabbage-like.

BUTTERCUP FAMILY **Globe Flower** *Trollius europaeus*. This strikingly handsome plant, 30–60cm high, is the only one in Europe with flowers which look like small yellow oranges. Its leaves are palmate with deeply cut lobes and resemble those of Meadow Buttercup (p. 32). It grows in damp grassy places in hills and on mountain rock ledges in Scotland, Wales, northern England and NW Ireland. It flowers from May–August and is sometimes seen in gardens.

BUTTERCUP FAMILY **Marsh Marigold** or
Kingcup *Caltha palustris*. This large stout
plant is widespread and locally common in
damp woods, marshy meadows and other
wet places. It is characterised by 5cm-wide
buttercup-like flowers, with bright glossy
yellow sepals but no petals, that appear from
March–June; hollow stems that grow to
30–45cm high but may creep along the
ground in hill districts; glossy, dark green
kidney-shaped leaves; and in summer heads
of claw-like seed-pods.

BUTTERCUP FAMILY **1 Bulbous Buttercup** *Ranunculus bulbosus*, **2 Meadow Buttercup** *R. acris*, **3 Creeping Buttercup** *R. repens*. These are the 3 commonest British buttercups. It is the first 2 that turn the spring meadows bright yellow, somewhat to the dismay of the farmer, whose cattle can be poisoned by eating too many. Bulbous Buttercup is shorter than Meadow Buttercup, has distinctive, down-turned sepals and a bulbous rootstock; it prefers limy soils. Creeping Buttercup has creeping runners and grows in damp places, often as a garden weed; it may flower into autumn and occasionally through mild winters.

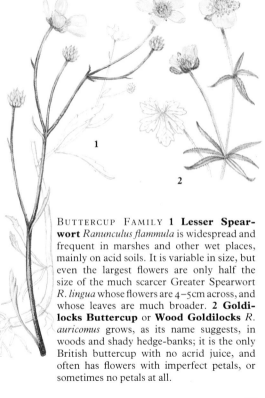

BUTTERCUP FAMILY **1 Lesser Spear-wort** *Ranunculus flammula* is widespread and frequent in marshes and other wet places, mainly on acid soils. It is variable in size, but even the largest flowers are only half the size of the much scarcer Greater Spearwort *R. lingua* whose flowers are 4–5cm across, and whose leaves are much broader. **2 Goldilocks Buttercup** or **Wood Goldilocks** *R. auricomus* grows, as its name suggests, in woods and shady hedge-banks; it is the only British buttercup with no acrid juice, and often has flowers with imperfect petals, or sometimes no petals at all.

BUTTERCUP FAMILY **Hepatica** *Hepatica nobilis*, a low-growing relative of the anemones, is not infrequent in gardens and sometimes escapes from them but on the Continent grows in woods and scrub on limy soils. Its untoothed three-lobed leaves are evergreen and purplish below. The solitary flowers, 15–25mm across, usually blue-purple but sometimes pink or white, appear in March and April. At first sight it appears to have both petals and sepals, but in fact there are no petals, and the coloured sepals have three sepal-like bracts just below them.

BUTTERCUP FAMILY **Yellow Anemone** *Anemone ranunculoides* grows like Hepatica in gardens and sometimes becomes established in shrubberies and other shady places outside them. On the Continent it grows quite commonly in woods. The deeply palmated lobes of its leaves are like those of the Wood Anemone (p. 36), and its usually solitary bright yellow flowers, 15–20mm across and appearing March–May, are very like those of a buttercup except that they are not glossy. Like all anemones it has no petals, but 5–8 coloured sepals.

Buttercup Family **1 Lesser Celandine** *Ranunculus ficaria* is one of the earliest spring flowers in Britain, appearing in hedge-banks at the end of mild Januaries in the south. It is no relation of Greater Celandine (p. 41). One form has small bulbils at the base of the leaves. **2 Wood Anemone** or **Windflower** *Anemone nemorosa* appears in late March, carpeting woods at the same time as the Primrose (p. 119). Its white flowers are often purplish-pink on the back of the petals (which are actually sepals) and occasionally coloured all over.

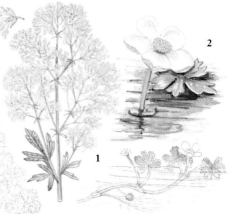

BUTTERCUP FAMILY **1 Common Meadow-rue** *Thalictrum flavum*. This tall plant has numerous garden relatives but grows completely wild in marshes and wet meadows and by streams. Its 4 petals are inconspicuous and the yellow fuzz of the flowers is due to the stamens. It flowers from June–August, mainly in the south and east. **2 Water Crowfoot** *Ranunculus aquatilis*. This is a group of very variable white-flowered buttercups that grows in wet mud, shallow water and strongly flowing streams. The leaves may be ivy-shaped and floating, or very finely divided and submerged, or both. It flowers from April–September.

1

2

Poppy Family **1 Yellow Corydalis** *Corydalis lutea* grows on village walls throughout England and Wales but is scarcer towards northern Scotland. Its leaves are twice pinnate and greyish beneath; it flowers from May to the autumn. **2 Common Fumitory** *Fumaria officinalis* is a common weed that owes its name (from the French) to the smoky appearance its greyish foliage gives the ground when it grows in quantity. The flowers may be pink or white and appear from late April to the autumn.

Poppy Family **1 Common Poppy** *Papaver rhoeas*. This, the commonest of the 4 native British poppies, has deep scarlet petals, often with a black patch at the base, and globular seed-pods; it flowers from June to the autumn. **2 Long-headed Poppy** *P. dubium* is rather less common in England and Wales but more frequent in Scotland, especially in the north. Its smaller, paler flowers, with no black patch at the base of the petals, appear from late May to early autumn and its seed-pods are elongated. Both species grow on roadsides and waste ground.

POPPY FAMILY **Yellow Horned Poppy**
Glaucium flavum. A characteristic plant of
shingle beaches and other coastal sites, with
large (5–7cm) yellow flowers, silvery-grey
foliage and remarkably long seed-pods; the
pods, anything up to 30cm long, are indeed
the longest of any British or European plant.
It is widespread and locally frequent all round
the coasts of England and Wales, from the
Wash to the Solway Firth; it is more local in
SW Scotland, Ireland and the Isle of Man.

POPPY FAMILY **Greater Celandine** *Chelidonium majus*. A medieval medicinal herb now found mainly in hedge-banks or on walls and waste ground in or near villages or isolated buildings in the country. Its only resemblance to Lesser Celandine (p. 36) is that it has yellow flowers and appears in spring. The name derives from the Greek for swallow, *chelidon*, which also appears in spring (but then so do many other birds and wild flowers!).

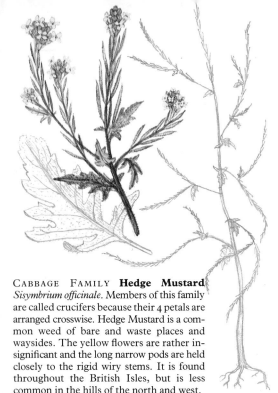

CABBAGE FAMILY **Hedge Mustard**
Sisymbrium officinale. Members of this family
are called crucifers because their 4 petals are
arranged crosswise. Hedge Mustard is a common weed of bare and waste places and
waysides. The yellow flowers are rather in-
significant and the long narrow pods are held
closely to the rigid wiry stems. It is found
throughout the British Isles, but is less
common in the hills of the north and west.

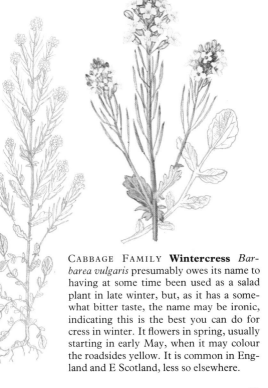

CABBAGE FAMILY **Wintercress** *Barbarea vulgaris* presumably owes its name to having at some time been used as a salad plant in late winter, but, as it has a somewhat bitter taste, the name may be ironic, indicating this is the best you can do for cress in winter. It flowers in spring, usually starting in early May, when it may colour the roadsides yellow. It is common in England and E Scotland, less so elsewhere.

43

CABBAGE FAMILY **1 Great Yellowcress**
Rorippa amphibia is a tall waterside plant with
globular seed-pods **(1a)**, found mainly in
the Midlands and SE England. **2 Creeping
Yellowcress** *R. sylvestris* is much smaller
with flowers half the size, and elongated pods
(2a); it grows on damp and bare ground, in
most places except in the north of Scotland.
3 Marsh Yellowcress *R. palustris* has smaller flowers still and dumpy pods **(3a)** and
grows on both damp and dry bare ground.

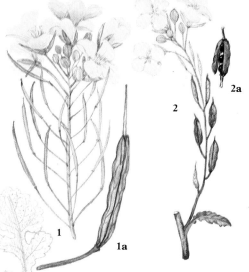

CABBAGE FAMILY **1 Wild Turnip** or
Bargeman's Cabbage *Brassica rapa* is a
common plant along river banks in many
parts of England and Wales, also an escape
from cultivation on waste ground every-
where. The wild plant does not have so swollen a root as the cultivated form; its seed-pod
(1a) is long and thin. **2 Black Mustard** *B.
nigra*, a close relative, grows in similar places,
has smaller flowers and a shorter pod **(2a)**.

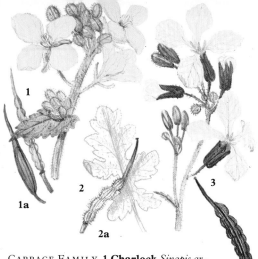

CABBAGE FAMILY **1 Charlock** *Sinapis arvensis* is a common wayside weed, now less often seen in cornfields because of modern pesticides. **2 White Mustard** *S. alba*, the partner of cress in sandwiches, is similar, but prefers chalky soils and has pinnate leaves **(2)** and a longer beak to the seed-pod **(2a)** than that of Charlock **(1a)**. **3 Wild Radish** *Raphanus raphanistrum* may have either pale yellow or whitish flowers, beaded pods **(3a)** and leaves like the garden radish. It is a common weed.

46

CABBAGE FAMILY **Cuckoo Flower** or **Lady's Smock** *Cardamine pratensis*. A common plant of damp meadows and marshy places that owes one of its names to starting to flower when the cuckoo arrives and the other doubtless to a favourite colour for ladies' smocks in the Middle Ages. The flowers may in fact be either lilac or white. It grows throughout Great Britain and Ireland, from the Scillies to the northernmost Shetlands.

fruit

CABBAGE FAMILY **Garlic Mustard** or **Jack by the Hedge** *Alliaria petiolata*. A very common white-flowered hedgerow plant, also growing in dampish woods, throughout England, Wales and eastern Scotland; less common in Ireland and SW Scotland. It flowers in spring, starting in mid-April. Its leaves are heart-shaped and have long stalks; they smell quite strongly of garlic when bruised.

CABBAGE FAMILY **Watercress** *Nasturtium officinale*. One of the few medieval salad plants whose use has survived widely to the present day. There is no difference between the wild and the cultivated plants, except that there are actually 2 closely similar species and their hybrid, and it is the hybrid that is most often cultivated. Its leaves turn bronzy in cold weather. The wild plant grows throughout the British Isles in shallow fresh water and on wet mud, flowering June–October.

CABBAGE FAMILY **Sea Rocket** *Cakile maritima* is
one of the few wild flowers that grow along the
edges of sandy shores nearest to the high tide mark;
other species are Sea Sandwort (p. 20) and the
slightly prickly Sea Saltwort *Salsola kali*, which has
tiny inconspicuous green flowers. Sea Rocket has the
4 crosswise petals typical of the Cabbage or Crucifer
Family; it is lilac-purple in colour and produces
globular seed-pods. It flowers from June–August.
Rocket is an old word for salad plants.

CABBAGE FAMILY Scurvy-grasses *Cochlearia* are so called because their vitamin C content helps to prevent the scurvy that used to afflict seamen who had no access to fresh fruit or vegetables. **1 Common Scurvy-grass** *C. officinalis* has fleshy heart-shaped leaves; the upper ones are unstalked; it flowers from April–August. **2 Danish Scurvy-grass** *C. danica* has stalked upper leaves, usually lilac flowers and appears as early as January in sheltered spots. Both scurvy-grasses grow on banks by the sea.

CABBAGE FAMILY **1 Hairy Bittercress**
Cardamine hirsuta is a very common weed in
garden beds and other bare and waste places.
It starts to flower in March, oíten earlier in
mild winters and produces long narrow seed-
pods. **2 Shepherd's Purse** *Capsella bursa-
pastoris* is an even commoner early-flowering
weed with triangular seed-pods supposedly
shaped like the purses carried by shepherds in
days gone by. Its leaves are very variable in
shape and may be well or only slightly toothed
or not toothed at all.

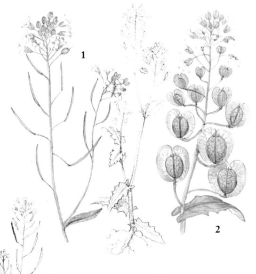

CABBAGE FAMILY **1 Thale Cress** *Arabidopsis thaliana* is a common early-flowering weed like those opposite. It can be distinguished from Hairy Bittercress by its undivided leaves and from Shepherd's Purse by its long narrow seed-pods. **2 Field Pennycress** *Thlaspi arvense* is a weed more frequently found on arable land. It can be identified by its large, almost circular flattened seed-pods, not unlike a penny; it flowers from late April–August.

CABBAGE FAMILY **Hoary Cress** *Cardaria draba* is now a common plant of waste ground in SE England, and widely scattered elsewhere. It is believed to have originated from mattresses, presumably containing the seeds of the plant, from the military expedition to Walcheren in the Low Countries in 1809 which were thrown on the ground in the Isle of Thanet in Kent.

1

2

MIGNONETTE FAMILY **1 Wild Mignon-ette** *Reseda lutea* is very like a garden mignonette, but not fragrant. It flowers from May onwards in rather bare places on chalk and limestone soils in England, Wales and eastern Scotland. **2 Weld** *R. luteola* is much taller and grows on all kinds of bare and waste ground over a wider area. It produces a yellow dye, which was much favoured by the Romans for wedding garments.

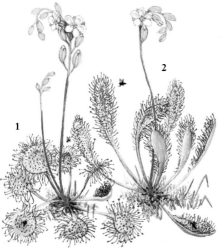

SUNDEW FAMILY **1 Round-leaved Sundew**
Drosera rotundifolia. A curious little plant, whose
basal rosette of almost circular leaves is covered with
sticky red hairs which can curve inwards to trap and
digest flies and other small insects. It is widespread
and locally common in bogs and on wet heaths and
moors; flowering June–August. **2 Great Sundew**
D. anglica is taller and has elongated leaves. Oblong-
leaved Sundew *D. intermedia* is smaller than Great
Sundew and has shorter leaves, a flowering stem
arising from below the rosette instead of from the
middle, and is commoner in the south.

STONECROP FAMILY **Navelwort** or **Wall Pennywort** *Umbilicus rupestris* is a succulent with circular (hence 'pennywort') leaves, which have a dimple in the centre, and almost tubular greenish bell-like flowers from June–August. It varies greatly in size from 5–7cm high on walls to 30cm or more on moist shady rocks. It is commonest in SW England, Wales and southern Ireland.

57

STONECROP FAMILY Stonecrops
Sedum are characterised by thick fleshy
leaves and a liking for dry places. **1 Biting
Stonecrop** *S. acre* is so named because of
the sharp taste of its leaves when chewed.
It is often found in gardens, as well as wild
on rocks and bare ground, on limy soils; its
bright yellow 5-petalled flowers appear
from May–July. **2 English Stonecrop**
S. anglicum prefers more acid soils and is
at its best on cliff tops in the west. Its white
flowers appear from June–September,
and its leaves often turn red.

SAXIFRAGE FAMILY Saxifrages *Saxifraga* derive their curious name – it means stone-breaking – from a supposed capacity to dissolve the stones in human bladders, but are rarely prescribed by the National Health Service! **1 Meadow Saxifrage** *S. granulata* is the largest-flowered species found in Britain and appears from April–June in grassy places. **2 Rue-leaved Saxifrage** *S. tridactylites* is the smallest British species and may be only a few centimetres high. It grows on walls, rocks and other dry bare spots, especially on limy soils, and flowers from April–May; its three-fingered (hence the Latin name) leaves are often reddish.

SAXIFRAGE FAMILY **Opposite-leaved Golden Saxifrage** *Chrysosplenium oppositifolium* forms a mat of roundish leaves in damp shady places, its small petalless green flowers appearing from March (February in the warm south-west) to May; widespread and locally common. It is distinguished from the much less common Alternate-leaved Golden Saxifrage *C. alternifolium*, which has larger, yellower flowerheads, by its flowering stems which have opposite pairs of leaves instead of alternate, one or no leaves. The Opposite-leaved Golden Saxifrage is quite unlike the saxifrages proper.

PARNASSUS-GRASS FAMILY **Grass of Parnassus** *Parnassia palustris*. A distinctive and beautiful flower, always solitary and looking like a graceful white buttercup, in marshes, fens and damp hollows on sand dunes. Locally common in Scotland, western Ireland and NW England, it is distinctly scarce in the rest of England and Wales, except in East Anglia; its flowering period is from July to September.

ROSE FAMILY **1 Meadowsweet** *Filipendula ulmaria*. The creamy fragrant flowers of Meadowsweet adorn ditches, watersides and marshes all over the country from June–October, but always in damp or wet places. Its pinnate leaves have 2–5 pairs of leaflets and are silvery below. **2 Dropwort** *F. vulgaris* is its downland counterpart, with similar but smaller clusters of flowers and up to 20 pairs of leaflets, not silvery beneath; it always grows in dry grassy places, on limy soils.

ROSE FAMILY **Agrimony** *Agrimonia eupatoria*. One of the commonest British grassland plants, this softly hairy perennial has pinnate leaves, the larger leaflets interspersed with smaller ones, and a spike of rather small yellow flowers, appearing from June–September. Its close relative Fragrant Agrimony *A. procera* grows mainly on acid soils, is stouter, has more fragrant leaves, and larger, paler yellow flowers. It is only really frequent south of the Thames.

2

1

ROSE FAMILY **1 Salad Burnet** *Sanguisorba minor*. A common and characteristic plant of chalky grassland, whose pinnate leaves have a cucumber smell when crushed, hence their use in medieval salads. The tiny green flowers are petalless, and coloured only by the yellow stamens and red styles, which appear in different flowers from late April–August. **2 Great Burnet** *S. officinalis* is much taller, with oblong heads of deep red-purple flowers, appearing from June–September in damp grassland.

ROSE FAMILY **1 Lady's Mantle** *Alchemilla vulgaris*. A very variable plant of grassy places, its tiny greenish flowers are petalless and coloured only by their yellow stamens. They appear widespread, May–September, but rather local in East Anglia and south of the Thames. **2 Alpine Lady's Mantle** *A. alpina* is a mountain plant, very common in the Scottish Highlands and the Lake District, but rare in the southern half of Ireland. Its leaves are silvery beneath, and unlike those of its commoner relative are divided to the base.

ROSE FAMILY **1 Wild Strawberry** *Fragaria vesca*. Easily recognisable as a miniature Garden Strawberry *F.* ×*ananassa*, which itself often escapes onto waste ground. Widespread and common in open woods and grassy places, mainly on limy soils, flowering April–September. **2 Barren Strawberry** *Potentilla sterilis* grows in similar places, but flowers only March–May, and differs in having rather bluish-green, matt, less sharply veined leaves, gaps between the petals, and dry unstrawberry-like fruits.

ROSE FAMILY **1 Marsh Cinquefoil** *Potentilla palustris*. A not uncommon plant of wet swamps and fens, with striking dark purple star-like flowers appearing from May–July. Its grey-green pinnate leaves have 3–5 leaflets. **2 Water Avens** *Geum rivale* grows in similar but not quite so wet places, and on mountains, but has almost bell-like, drooping, pinkish-orange flowers, and pinnate leaves with a very large end lobe. Both are commoner in the north than in the south.

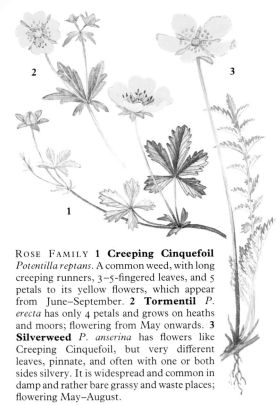

ROSE FAMILY **1 Creeping Cinquefoil**
Potentilla reptans. A common weed, with long
creeping runners, 3–5-fingered leaves, and 5
petals to its yellow flowers, which appear
from June–September. **2 Tormentil** *P.
erecta* has only 4 petals and grows on heaths
and moors; flowering from May onwards. **3
Silverweed** *P. anserina* has flowers like
Creeping Cinquefoil, but very different
leaves, pinnate, and often with one or both
sides silvery. It is widespread and common in
damp and rather bare grassy and waste places;
flowering May–August.

1

2

PEAFLOWER FAMILY **1 Dyer's Green-weed** *Genista tinctoria*. A locally frequent undershrub resembling a diminutive Broom *Sarothamnus scoparius* but with no thorns. It grows in grassland, heaths and open woods, flowering from June–August. It was once used to make a yellow dye, which, when mixed with woad (whose dye is blue) made a good green dye. **2 Petty Whin** *G. anglica* is a smaller, thorny plant, that grows on heaths and moors, especially among heather, and starts to flower earlier, sometimes in late April. It extends further north than Dyer's Greenweed into the Scottish Highlands. Neither grows in Ireland.

PEAFLOWER FAMILY **Birdsfoot Trefoil** *Lotus corniculatus*, one of the commonest grassland plants in Britain, is also popularly known as Eggs and Bacon because of its colour, and, more enigmatically, as Tom Thumb. The yellow, orange or reddish flowers appear from May–September. The leaves have 5 leaflets, 2 of which are bent back so that the plant appears to have trefoil leaves. The seed-pods are straight, in a head resembling the claws of a bird's foot – hence the name of the plant.

PEAFLOWER FAMILY **Greater Birdsfoot Trefoil** *Lotus uliginosus* grows in damp grass and flowers June–August. It is a larger version of the common Birdsfoot Trefoil (opposite), from which it can be distinguished by its erecter growth and broader leaflets, greyer beneath. In addition, it has more flowers in each head, the sepal teeth spread instead of being erect in bud, and the 2 upper ones at an acute, not an obtuse, angle.

PEAFLOWER FAMILY **1 Tufted Vetch**
Vicia cracca is found clambering by tendrils
over other vegetation in hedgerows, fens and
other grassy and bushy places; it flowers from
June–August and produces brown seed-
pods. **2 Bush Vetch** *V. sepium* can be distinguished from Tufted Vetch by the smaller
number of larger flowers which make up each
cluster; these flowers are duller purple and
the seed-pods are black. It grows in similar
but usually shady places and flowers from late
April–November.

1

2

PEAFLOWER FAMILY **1 Common
Vetch** *Vicia sativa* varies in size and
stoutness but always has 1–2 red-
purple flowers and tendrilled leaves;
large forms are cultivated. It grows in
disturbed ground and other bare or
thinly grassy places, and flowers from
April–September. **2 Smooth Tare**
V. tetrasperma has smaller, deep lilac
flowers and grows in similar but
grassier places; it flowers from
May–August.

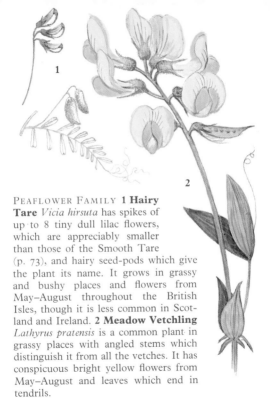

PEAFLOWER FAMILY **1 Hairy Tare** *Vicia hirsuta* has spikes of up to 8 tiny dull lilac flowers, which are appreciably smaller than those of the Smooth Tare (p. 73), and hairy seed-pods which give the plant its name. It grows in grassy and bushy places and flowers from May–August throughout the British Isles, though it is less common in Scotland and Ireland. **2 Meadow Vetchling** *Lathyrus pratensis* is a common plant in grassy places with angled stems which distinguish it from all the vetches. It has conspicuous bright yellow flowers from May–August and leaves which end in tendrils.

PEAFLOWER FAMILY **Sainfoin** *Onobrychis viciifolia* owes its name – from the French for 'wholesome hay' – to the fact that it was once widely used as a fodder crop. Most plants seen today are derived from this source, but there is a native form, semi-prostrate with deeper pink flowers, which is found especially on chalk in eastern England. Sainfoin is found in dry grassy and bare places on limy soils and flowers from June–September. It is a good honey plant.

PEAFLOWER FAMILY Rest-harrows *Ononis* are so called because their tough wiry stems used to impede harrows in the Middle Ages. **1 Common Rest-harrow** *O. repens* usually grows along the ground in dry grassy places and often on limy soils. It has trefoil leaves, hairs all over the stems and sometimes soft spines; it flowers from July–September. **2 Spiny Rest-harrow** *O. spinosa* is erecter, with sharper spines, 2 lines of hairs on the stems and flowers of a harder, reddish pink; it prefers neutral grassland.

PEAFLOWER FAMILY Melilots *Melilotus* have trefoil leaves and long spikes of small flowers; they grow in bare or sparsely grassy places and flower from June–September. The melilots are also good honey plants. **1 Ribbed Melilot** *M. officinalis* has yellow flowers and hairless brown seed-pods. **2 Tall Melilot** *M. altissima* has deeper yellow flowers than Ribbed Melilot, downy black seed-pods and prefers rather grassier places. **3 White Melilot** *M. alba* is grown as a fodder plant under the name of Bokhara Clover; it has white flowers and hairless brown pods.

PEAFLOWER FAMILY **1 Black Medick**
Medicago lupulina. One of a group of widespread small yellow-flowered peaflowers with
trefoil leaves, distinguished by its downy
stems, pointed leaflets and black fruits.
2 Lesser Trefoil *Trifolium dubium* is hairless,
has notched leaflets and dead brown flowers
enfolding its fruits. **3 Hop Trefoil** *T. campestris* is similar with larger flowerheads.
4 Spotted Medick *M. arabica* has black-
spotted leaves and few flowers in the head; it
grows in sandy places near the sea. The two
medicks flower April–September, and the
trefoils May–September.

Peaflower Family **1 Red Clover** *Trifolium pratense*. One of the commonest and most widespread wild plants in Britain. A tall variety is often cultivated and escapes onto roadsides and waste ground. **2 Strawberry Clover** *T. fragiferum* is rather local in grassland, especially near the sea, and has most distinctive strawberry-like fruiting heads. **3 Haresfoot Clover** *T. arvense* is easily told by its oblong flowerheads and grows in dry, rather bare sandy places, also often near the sea. Red Clover flowers May–September; the other 2 do not start till June.

1

2

PEAFLOWER FAMILY **1 White Clover**
Trifolium repens. The other common and
widespread British clover, also frequently cultivated under the names of Kentish or Wild
White Clover. It has creeping runners, leaves
with a whitish blotch, and its flowers may also
be pink or even purple. **2 Alsike Clover**
T. hybridum is another often cultivated clover
that escapes onto roadsides and waste ground.
It is taller and does not creep, its leaves never
have a whitish mark, and its flowers are
more often pink. Both flower from June–
September.

FLAX FAMILY **1 Fairy Flax** *Linum cathar-
ticum*. A characteristic plant of chalk and
limestone turf, best distinguished from the
rather similar chickweed-type plants of the
Pink Family (pp. 20–3) by having 5 petals;
flowering May–September. WOOD SOR-
REL FAMILY **2 Wood Sorrel** *Oxalis acetosella*. A widespread and common plant in
woods, which also appears on mountains. It is
unique among woodland plants in its com-
bination of solitary white bell-like flowers and
trefoil leaves; its flowering period is from
April–May.

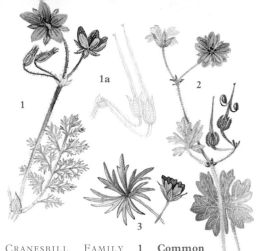

CRANESBILL FAMILY **1 Common Storksbill** *Erodium cicutarium*. A variable plant, with flowers not infrequently white, and a long beak on the fruit (**1a**), whence its name. Widespread and common in dry grassy and sandy places. **2 Dovesfoot Cranesbill** *Geranium molle* grows in similar places, but has quite different leaves and shorter fruits. **3 Cut-leaved Cranesbill** *G. dissectum* differs from Dovesfoot Cranesbill especially in its deeply cut leaves; more often as a weed of cultivation. All three flower from May–September.

CRANESBILL FAMILY **1 Meadow Cranes-bill** *Geranium pratense*. One of our hand-somest wild flowers, often adorning road verges in the Cotswolds and other limestone districts from June–August. Its fruits **(1a)** have the typical long beak that gives the plant its name. **2 Wood Cranesbill** *G. sylvaticum* is a more northern plant, also growing on mountains, which has smaller flowers, more mauve and less blue in colour, and somewhat less jagged leaves.

CRANESBILL FAMILY **Herb Robert** *Geranium robertianum*. A common woodland plant that also grows on hedge-banks, walls, rocks and shingle by the sea. It is rather strong-smelling and often the whole plant is suffused in red; sometimes, especially when it grows on shingle, it is almost prostrate. It starts to flower in April and continues until November. Its medieval name was *Herba Roberti* but it is not certain who is the Robert it commemorates; the Limestone Fern *Gymnocarpium robertianum* owes its Latin name to the fact that it has a smell which is rather like that of Herb Robert.

SPURGE FAMILY **Wood Spurge** *Euphorbia amygdaloides*. Spurges are characterised by their acrid milky juice and their curious petalless flowers. What look like petals are actually cup-like bracts; the real flowers lie within them, the males with a tiny anther and the females with 3 styles, often forked. Wood Spurge grows, as its name suggests, in and on the edge of woods and copses, in England and Wales, but not in Scotland. It is much commoner in the south. It flowers in April and May or sometimes at the end of March.

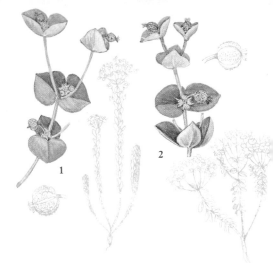

SPURGE FAMILY **1 Sea Spurge** *Euphorbia paralias*. A characteristic plant of dunes and sandy places by the sea, flowering June–August; its greyish leaves overlap up the stems. **2 Portland Spurge** *E. portlandica* grows on grassy cliffs as well, and flowers from April. It often turns red, and has narrower, minutely pointed leaves, with the midrib prominent beneath, which grow more loosely up the stem. Both are largely southern, extending north to Galloway on the west side of Britain, but only Sea Spurge grows between West Sussex and Norfolk.

SPURGE FAMILY **Sun Spurge** *Euphorbia helioscopia*. A very common weed of gardens and other bare and cultivated places, and the only common British spurge with toothed leaves. Its flowers are a much yellower green than Petty Spurge (p. 88), the other common garden-weed spurge. It flowers from April or May onward to the winter frosts, and may even flower right through a mild winter.

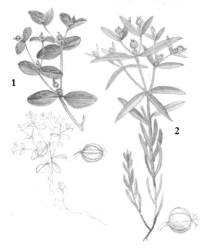

SPURGE FAMILY **1 Petty Spurge** *Euphorbia peplus*. With Sun Spurge (p. 87) this is the other common garden weed among native spurges. It has much greener flowerheads than Sun Spurge, and is less broadly spreading, but like Sun Spurge it can flower almost throughout the year. **2 Dwarf Spurge** *E. exigua* is a cornfield weed with much narrower leaves than Petty Spurge, and yellower flowers, which do not appear till late June. It is largely confined to the south and east of England, being rather sparse in Scotland, Wales and the SW peninsula.

BALSAM FAMILY **1 Indian Balsam** *Impatiens glandulifera*, from the Himalayas, is now common in much of England and Wales by fresh water and in dry, waste places. Its Chinese-lantern shaped dark or light pink flowers are unmistakable. **2 Orange Balsam** *I. capensis*, from North America, has smaller, bright orange flowers, and is increasing along southern and Midland rivers. **3 Touch-me-not Balsam** *I. noli-tangere*, very local in damp woods, has yellow flowers. All three flower July–September.

MILKWORT FAMILY **1 Common Milk-
wort** *Polygala vulgaris*. Milkworts have distinctive flowers, appearing May–August.
Common Milkwort has blue, mauve or white
flowers; it grows in grassy places; the leaves
are arranged alternately. **2 Heath Milkwort**
P. serpyllifolia has dark blue or dark pink
flowers, and leaves opposite; it grows on
heaths, moors and acid grassland. **3 Chalk
Milkwort** *P. calcarea* has clear gentian blue
flowers, leaves in a basal semi-rosette; it
grows in chalk grassland in S and E England.

MALLOW FAMILY **1 Common Mallow**
Malva sylvestris. A widespread and common
plant of farmyards and similar waste places, it
often grows at the foot of a wall; its bright
pinkish-purple flowers appear from June–
September. **2 Dwarf Mallow** *M. neglecta*
grows in similar places, but has much smaller,
pale lilac-purple or whitish flowers. Both of
these plants are much more commonly
found in the south, east and Midlands than
they are in the north and west of England and
in Scotland and Wales.

MALLOW FAMILY **Musk Mallow**
Malva moschata. A most attractive wild
flower, looking as if it had escaped from a
garden bed, but in fact perfectly native.
Its handsome rose-pink flowers appear in
July and August, a month later than Common Mallow (p. 91), from which it is also
distinguished by its deeply and finely cut
leaves. None of these three mallows produces the sweetmeat marshmallow, which
is made from the roots of the Marsh
Mallow *Althaea officinalis*, a rather uncommon saltmarsh plant.

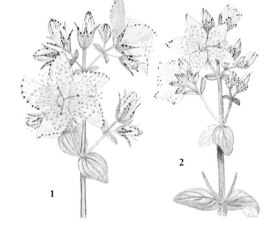

St John's Wort Family **1 Perforate St John's Wort** *Hypericum perforatum* is generally the commonest of the St John's Worts; its name refers to the numerous translucent dots which can be seen on its leaves. It is hairless and its flowers have petals edged with black dots; it grows in grassy places and scrub. Introduced into Australia and New Zealand, it has become a pestilential weed. **2 Hairy St John's Wort** *H. hirsutum* is hairy and has paler yellow flowers which are sometimes red-veined; it grows in woods, scrub and shady places, especially on limy soils. Both of these St John's Worts flower in July and August.

ST JOHN'S WORT FAMILY **1 Square-stalked St John's Wort** *Hypericum tetra-pterum*. The chief distinguishing characteristics of this marshland and waterside St John's Wort are its square stems and pale yellow flowers. **2 Slender St John's Wort** *H. pulchrum* is the most attractive member of the genus in Britain, with its delicate stems and its red-tinged, deeper yellow flowers; it grows in open woods and heathy places on acid soils. It is much the commonest St John's Wort in the north and west of Britain. Both species flower in July and August.

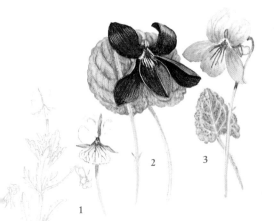

VIOLET FAMILY **1 Field Pansy** *Viola arvensis*. A widespread and common weed of cultivation, whose creamy flowers often have patches of yellow or violet, vary greatly in size, and appear from April onwards and occasionally through mild winters. **2 Sweet Violet** *V. odorata* is easily told by the sweet smell of its often white flowers, which appear in March and April (February in the mild SW) in hedge-banks and other shady places. **3 Hairy Violet** *V. hirta* is not fragrant, and has bluer-purple flowers from March–May in chalk and limestone grassland; its leaves are longer and narrower than Sweet Violet.

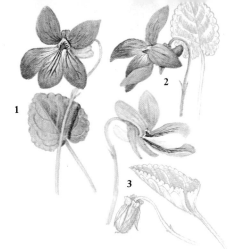

VIOLET FAMILY **1 Common Dog Violet** *Viola riviniana*. Generally the commonest dog violet, so called because being unscented they are fit only for dogs. The flowers appear from late March–May, with a curved notched creamy spur, in woods and grassy places, and on mountains. **2 Early Dog Violet** *V. reichenbachiana* appears a fortnight earlier, mainly in woods on chalk in the south; the flowers are narrower, with a straight unnotched purple spur. **3 Heath Dog Violet** *V. canina* has longer, narrower leaves, blue-purple flowers at the end of April, and grows in sandier places.

1

2

3

VIOLET FAMILY **1 Wild Pansy** or **Heartsease** *Viola tricolor*. A variable plant whose short-spurred flowers may be yellow, purple or a mixture, measures about 15mm across, and appear from April–August in cultivated and grassy places. **2 Seaside Pansy** *V. curtisii* is an attractive, always yellow form that grows in sand dunes, mainly in the north and west. **3 Mountain Pansy** *V. lutea* has much larger flowers, often 2.5cm or more long, with a much longer spur, appearing in May and growing in short turf in the north and west, mainly in hilly districts.

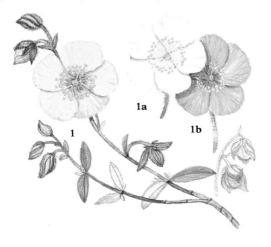

ROCK ROSE FAMILY **1 Common Rock-rose**
Helianthemum nummularium. Much the commonest
rock-rose, this attractive undershrub, with its leaves
downy white beneath and its bright yellow flowers
appearing from May–August, grows in chalk and
limestone turf and on mountains throughout Britain,
but more commonly in the south and east. Its flowers
may also occasionally be white **(1a)** or a deeper yellow
(1b). The white ones must not be confused with the
rare White Rock-rose *H. appenninum*, a speciality of
the limestone of S. Devon and N. Somerset, which
has leaves which are downy grey on both sides.

YAM FAMILY **1 Black Bryony** *Tamus communis* is a non-woody climber, twining without tendrils, allied to the lilies and orchids. It has shiny heart-shaped leaves, small 6-petalled flowers in May–August, and red berries. It grows in hedges and scrub throughout England and Wales, except in the far north. MELON FAMILY **2 White Bryony** *Bryonia cretica* is a quite different plant, climbing with tendrils. It has matt, ivy-shaped leaves, larger, 5-petalled flowers, and a more southerly distribution than Black Bryony.

WILLOW-HERB FAMILY **Large-flowered Evening Primrose** *Oenothera erythrosepala*. A garden plant from North America which has established itself widely on waste ground, sand dunes and similar bare places. There are several species at large in Britain, but this is the commonest and is distinguished by the numerous red-based hairs on its stems and fruits, as well as by its 7cm-wide flowers, which appear from late June–September.

WILLOW-HERB FAMILY **Enchanter's Nightshade** *Circaea lutetiana*. A common weed in shady gardens, also often found carpeting woodlands, except in the north of Scotland; it flowers from June–August and is the only common wild flower in Britain to have only 2 petals. Its fruits are covered in hooked bristles. It takes its name from the famous enchantress Circe, with whom Ulysses clashed in the *Odyssey*, apparently because in classical Greece its root was used as a charm.

WILLOW-HERB FAMILY **Rosebay Willow-herb** *Epilobium angustifolium*. Widespread and common in woods and on waste ground, it became very common on the bombed sites of cities during and after World War II, when it was often miscalled Loosestrife (p. 105). Unlike other willow-herbs its flowers, which appear from June–September, have unequal petals.

WILLOW-HERB FAMILY **Great Willow-herb** *Epilobium hirsutum*. The tallest British willow-herb and the only one with flowers 2cm across, it is very common in damp places, especially by streams and road-side ditches, throughout Britain, except that it thins out markedly as you go north in Scotland. Its faint fragrance has earned it the folk name of Codlins and Cream. Like other willow-herbs, it has silky plumes of hair attached to its seeds.

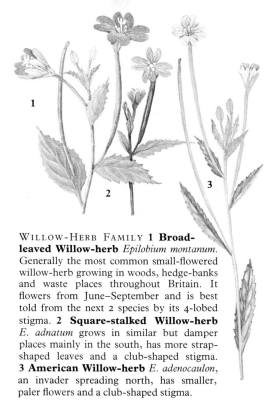

WILLOW-HERB FAMILY **1 Broad-leaved Willow-herb** *Epilobium montanum*. Generally the most common small-flowered willow-herb growing in woods, hedge-banks and waste places throughout Britain. It flowers from June–September and is best told from the next 2 species by its 4-lobed stigma. **2 Square-stalked Willow-herb** *E. adnatum* grows in similar but damper places mainly in the south, has more strap-shaped leaves and a club-shaped stigma. **3 American Willow-herb** *E. adenocaulon*, an invader spreading north, has smaller, paler flowers and a club-shaped stigma.

LOOSESTRIFE FAMILY **Purple Loose-strife** *Lythrum salicaria*. A most handsome plant when growing in quantity by a lake or stream, in marshes or fens. It is less common in Scotland. Its 6-petalled bright purple flowers, which appear from June–August, are quite different from the 4-petalled ones of Rosebay Willow-herb (p. 102), with which it is sometimes confused. Its name has a curious origin, being derived from a King of Sicily called Lysimachius, but adapted through its Greek meaning to make it a plant that can be used to quieten a quarrel.

UMBELLIFER FAMILY **Sanicle** *Sanicula euro-*
paea. This flower, sometimes called Wood Sanicle
because it grows almost exclusively in woods (especially beechwoods), is a most untypical umbellifer,
but nevertheless does have its white or pinkish
flowers arranged in the umbrella shape more easily
recognised in the species on pp. 108–16. It flowers
from May to early July, and produces fruits with
hooked spines. Its name derives from a Latin word
for healing, reflecting its former medicinal use.

UMBELLIFER FAMILY **Sea Holly** *Eryngium maritimum*. Another, even more atypical umbellifer than Sanicle (opposite), with almost globular heads. It is a striking and unmistakable plant, with its blue-green prickly leaves and handsome powder-blue flower-heads, appearing in July–August. It is widespread round the coast, most often on sand, but sometimes also on shingle. It seems to have become extinct on the east coast north of Flamborough Head, Yorkshire, and was never found in the north of Scotland.

UMBELLIFER FAMILY **1 Cow Parsley**
Anthriscus sylvestris. One of the commonest
umbellifers, being the Queen Anne's Lace
that lines countless roadsides in April and
May, except for parts of the Scottish Highlands. **2 Rough Chervil** *Chaerophyllum
temulentum* flowers 4–6 weeks later, and is not
so abundant in the hedgerows, nor so frequent in Scotland. It differs especially in its
solid, more or less spotted stems.

1   2

UMBELLIFER FAMILY **1 Upright Hedge Parsley** *Torilis japonica*. This slenderer but wirier plant takes over in the hedge-banks when the two umbellifers opposite are gone, in July and August. Its unspotted stems are roughly hairy, and its flowers often pinkish. **2 Wild Carrot** *Daucus carota* is unmistakable with its 3-forked or pinnate lower bracts around the flowerhead, which appears from June–September; grows commonly in grassy places, especially on limy soils.

UMBELLIFER FAMILY **1 Burnet Saxifrage** *Pimpinella saxifraga*. Neither a burnet nor a saxifrage, it was once believed to 'break stones', ie to cure stone in humans. 'Burnet' derives from the resemblance of its lower leaves to Salad Burnet (p. 64). It grows in dry grassland, especially on limy soils and flowers June–October. **2 Pignut** or **Earthnut** *Conopodium majus* has an edible tuber beloved of pigs, flowers May–July and grows in drier woods and grassy places.

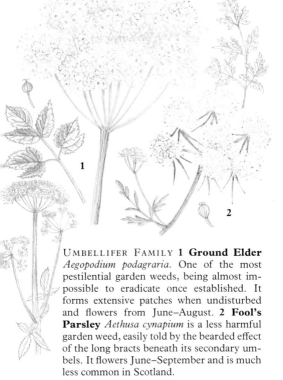

UMBELLIFER FAMILY **1 Ground Elder**
Aegopodium podagraria. One of the most
pestilential garden weeds, being almost im-
possible to eradicate once established. It
forms extensive patches when undisturbed
and flowers from June–August. **2 Fool's
Parsley** *Aethusa cynapium* is a less harmful
garden weed, easily told by the bearded effect
of the long bracts beneath its secondary um-
bels. It flowers June–September and is much
less common in Scotland.

UMBELLIFER FAMILY **Hogweed** *Heracleum sphondylium*. The commonest large white umbellifer of the fields and roadsides from June into the autumn. A stout, coarse plant with white, or occasionally pink flowers and hollow stems up to 3m high. The alien Giant Hogweed *H. mantegazzianum*, which can be poisonous to the touch, grows to 5m and is now widely established in Britain.

UMBELLIFER FAMILY **Wild Angelica**
Angelica sylvestris. The latest to flower
(July–September) of the large white umbellifers, it grows in damp woods. Its flowers are
often pinkish and its 1–1½m stems usually
purple, with inflated leaf-stalks. Garden Angelica *A. archangelica*, whose aromatic stems
are the source of the sweetmeat, is naturalised
by the Thames at Kew, Surrey, and in various
other places. It has green stems and greenish
or yellowish flowers.

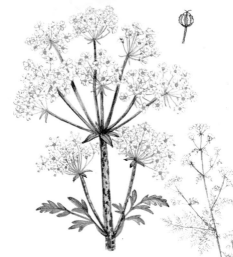

UMBELLIFER FAMILY **Hemlock** *Conium maculatum*. One of Britain's most poisonous wild plants, whose juice was used to kill the famous Greek philosopher Socrates. A tall plant, to 2m, it combines purple-spotted stems with a nauseous smell when crushed, and white flowers which appear from June–August. It grows in dampish places, by roads and streams, and on waste ground. Many other white umbellifers are liable to be loosely called 'hemlock'.

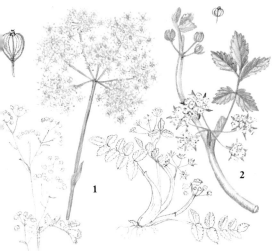

UMBELLIFER FAMILY **1 Wild Parsnip**
Pastinaca sativa. Like a smaller Hogweed (p.
112), but with yellow flowers; the stems and
leaves are pungent when crushed. A close
relative of the cultivated parsnip, it flowers
from July–September in bare and grassy
places on limy soils. **2 Fool's Watercress**
Apium nodiflorum is fortunately not poisonous, so if fools do mistake it for Watercress
(p. 49), which has quite different flowers, no
harm is done; grows in ditches and streams
and flowers June–September.

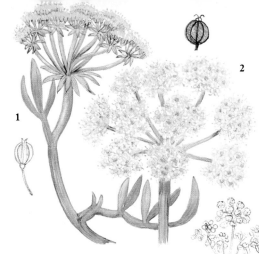

UMBELLIFER FAMILY **1 Rock Samphire** *Crithmum maritimum*. This edible, but now rarely eaten, plant is the samphire to which Shakespeare refers in *King Lear*: 'halfway down hangs one that gathers samphire, dreadful trade'. It grows on maritime cliffs and rocks and flowers from July–October. **2 Alexanders** *Smyrnium olusatrum* is another medieval pot-herb. It is common in hedge-banks and on waste ground by the sea but rarely found inland. It flowers late March–June.

HEATH FAMILY **1 Heather** or **Ling** *Calluna vulgaris* is the plant that turns moors and heaths purple every August; it is also found in bogs, open woods and on old dunes. White heather is a variant. **2 Bell Heather** *Erica cinerea* has larger and brighter purple flowers from June–September. **3 Cross-leaved Heath** *E. tetralix* has distinctive pink flowers which appear from June–August and grows in damp or wet places on heaths and moors and in bogs.

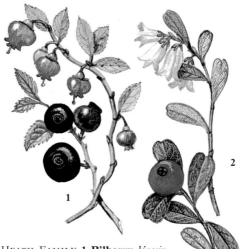

HEATH FAMILY **1 Bilberry** *Vaccinium myrtillus*. A plant whose well-known black edible fruits have many names: Bilberry in the north of England, Whortlebury or Hurt in the south, Blaeberry in Scotland. It flowers April–May and is found on heaths and moors. **2 Cowberry** *Vaccinium vitis-idaea* can be told from Bilberry by its evergreen leaves, creeping habit, whiter flowers and edible berries which turn red when ripe. It is locally common in the north and west and flowers May–June.

1

2

PRIMROSE FAMILY

1 Cowslip *Primula veris*. A well-known flower with fragrant flowers resembling a small garden Polyanthus. It grows mostly on chalk or limestone grassland and flowers in April and May. **2 Primrose** *P. vulgaris* is one of the best loved flowers in Britain and the favourite of the great statesman Disraeli; his birthday, 19 April, is still called Primrose Day. It is locally common in woods and scrub and on sea cliffs and railway banks; it flowers from January in mild winters to May or June.

PRIMROSE FAMILY **1 False Oxlip** *Primula × variabilis*. This hybrid between Primrose and Cowslip (p. 119) is often confused with the true Oxlip, but is more widespread, occurring singly wherever the 2 parents grow together; its flowers are deeper yellow than true Oxlip but paler than Cowslip. **2 Oxlip** *P. elatior* is a very local plant confined to a few oakwoods south and west of Cambridge where it grows in quantity and replaces the Primrose. It closely resembles the garden Polyanthus and flowers April–May. Its leaves are abruptly narrowed at the base.

PRIMROSE FAMILY **1 Yellow Loosestrife** *Lysimachia vulgaris*. A tall plant which grows in marshes and by water and flowers July–August. Similar plants growing in drier places are probably garden escapes, usually *L. punctata*. **2 Creeping Jenny** *L. nummularia* is a familiar cottage garden plant with rather bell-shaped flowers from June–August; it grows in damp woods and grassy places but is rare in Scotland and Ireland. **3 Yellow Pimpernel** *L. nemorum* is a fairly common plant in damp woods; its open star-like flowers appear May–August throughout the British Isles.

PRIMROSE FAMILY **1 Bog Pimpernel**
Anagallis tenella is a small creeping plant
with charming little bell-like, pink flowers
from June–August; it is found in bogs, fens
and damp grassy or mossy places. **2 Sea
Milkwort** *Glaux maritima* is a small prostrate saltmarsh plant whose flowers have pale
pink sepals, but no petals, and appear in
June–July. **3 Scarlet Pimpernel** *Anagallis
arvensis* is a common weed of bare places,
known as Poor Man's Weatherglass because it
closes its flowers when the sun goes in.

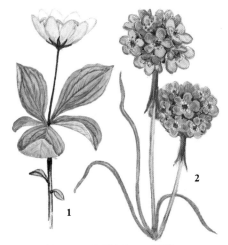

PRIMROSE FAMILY **1 Chickweed Wintergreen**
Trientalis europaea has a single whorl of lanceolate
leaves just below its usually solitary white starlike
flowers, which appear May–August. It grows in pine
and other coniferous woods and on heathland. SEA-
LAVENDER FAMILY **2 Thrift** or **Sea Pink** *Armeria maritima* is a common seaside plant whose
leafless stems bear heads of flowers in every shade of
pink, making a marvellous show on cliffs and rocks
by the sea from April to autumn. It also grows in
saltmarshes, on some mountains, and in one or two
sandy districts inland.

SEA-LAVENDER FAMILY **1 Common Sea-lavender** *Limonium vulgare*. This is the plant that turns many saltmarshes into sheets of lilac-purple in July and August. It is quite unrelated to the true Lavender *Lavandula officinalis*, a Mediterranean plant of the Labiate Family. **2 Matted Sea-lavender** *Limonium bellidifolium* is a speciality of drier saltmarshes on the north coast of Norfolk, easily distinguished by the numerous zigzag barren branches below its flowering spikes. It flowers July–August.

BOGBEAN FAMILY **Bogbean** or **Buckbean** *Menyanthes trifoliata*. A striking aquatic plant whose trefoil leaves and conspicuous flower spikes both project above the water in the very wet bogs, fens and shallow lagoons where it grows in all parts of the British Isles. The flowers are pink outside but white inside, the petals being fringed inside with long white hairs; appearing May–June and followed by globular green fruits.

GENTIAN FAMILY **1 Common Centaury** *Centaurium erythraea* is a most attractive plant with its clusters of bright salmon-pink flowers appearing from June–August. It grows fairly commonly in dry grassy places and on sand dunes, though not in Scotland. **2 Yellow-wort** *Blackstonia perfoliata* is in many ways a yellow counterpart of Common Centaury but the whole plant is grey-green and the leaves are joined at the base. It is fairly frequent in chalk and limestone grassland and on dunes, but not in Scotland.

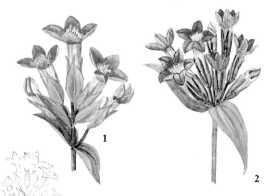

GENTIAN FAMILY **1 Field Gentian**
Gentianella campestris is an attractive bluish-purple gentian distinguished from the commoner Autumn Gentian by its taller and bushier growth and by larger, paler flowers, with petals and other parts nearly always in 4s, which appear in July. It grows on grassland and dunes, mainly in the north. **2 Autumn Gentian** or **Felwort** *G. amarella* is the commonest British gentian and is locally frequent in chalk and limestone grassland and on dunes throughout the British Isles. The dull purple or sometimes whitish flowers, with petals and other parts in 5s, appear in August–September. Its name means 'plant of open country'.

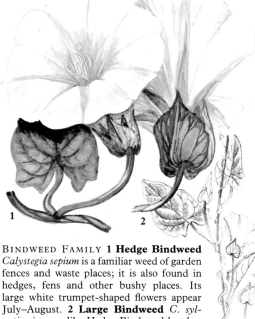

BINDWEED FAMILY **1 Hedge Bindweed**
Calystegia sepium is a familiar weed of garden
fences and waste places; it is also found in
hedges, fens and other bushy places. Its
large white trumpet-shaped flowers appear
July–August. **2 Large Bindweed** *C. sylvatica* is very like Hedge Bindweed but has
larger flowers with sepal-like bracts which
completely enfold the base. It is a garden
escape from North America that is now very
widespread in and near towns and villages.

BINDWEED FAMILY **Sea Bindweed** *Calystegia soldanella* is one of the most characteristic plants of bare sand dunes and is also occasionally to be found on shingle by the sea. Its creeping stems bear rows of kidney-shaped leaves and trumpet-shaped flowers; these are bright pink with white stripes and appear from June–August. It grows all round the coast of England and Wales, but is very local in Scotland, and in Ireland is to be found mainly on the east coast.

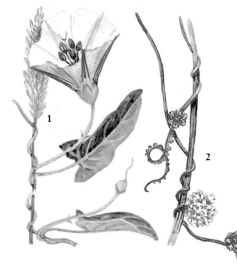

BINDWEED FAMILY **1 Field Bindweed** *Convolvulus arvensis*. One of the gardener's chief banes, despite its attractive white or pink trumpet-shaped flowers; being a perennial it is hard to eradicate, and its long stems twine anti-clockwise around other plants. It is also found in hedge-banks and on farmland; flowering June–September. **2 Dodder** *Cuscuta epithymum* is an extraordinary parasite which makes a dense network of red twining stems in July and August especially on heather and gorse.

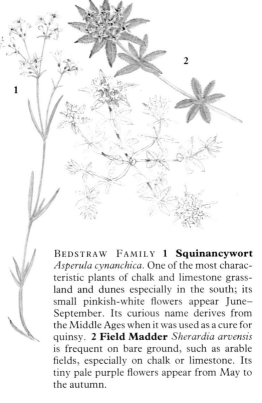

BEDSTRAW FAMILY **1 Squinancywort** *Asperula cynanchica*. One of the most characteristic plants of chalk and limestone grassland and dunes especially in the south; its small pinkish-white flowers appear June–September. Its curious name derives from the Middle Ages when it was used as a cure for quinsy. **2 Field Madder** *Sherardia arvensis* is frequent on bare ground, such as arable fields, especially on chalk or limestone. Its tiny pale purple flowers appear from May to the autumn.

BEDSTRAW FAMILY **Woodruff** or **Sweet Woodruff** *Galium odoratum*. This is one of the plants that carpets the spring woodlands. It grows in fairly deep shade and especially in ashwoods, beechwoods and other woods on chalk and limestone throughout the British Isles. The flowers are white, forming loose heads, and appear from April–June. Its leaves are arranged in whorls. The fruits are covered with hooked bristles. At one time Woodruff was used for flavouring in cooking, hence its alternative name.

BEDSTRAW FAMILY **1 Crosswort** *Cruc-iata laevipes* is widespread in grassy and bushy places on chalk and limestone soils but is very rare in Ireland. The leaves, in whorls of 4, are yellowish-green and the pale yellow flowers appear from April–June. **2 Lady's Bedstraw** *Galium verum*. All bedstraws, as their name suggests, were used for bedding in the Middle Ages; this one was evidently for ladies. It grows in dry grassy places and its yellow flowers appear from July–September.

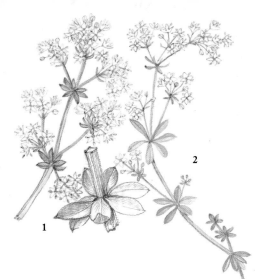

BEDSTRAW FAMILY **1 Hedge Bedstraw**
Galium mollugo. A common white-flowered
bedstraw that scrambles over other vegetation on hedge-banks and in dry grassy
places, especially on limy soils; it is less common in the north. It flowers July–August. **2
Heath Bedstraw** *G. saxatilis* is smaller and
slenderer than Hedge Bedstraw. It prefers
grassy and heathy places on acid soils and
flowers a month earlier, in June.

BEDSTRAW FAMILY **1 Common Marsh Bedstraw** *Galium palustre* is similar to Hedge Bedstraw (opposite) but less robust. It grows in wet and marshy places and flowers June–August. **2 Cleavers** or **Goosegrass** *G. aparine* is by far the commonest bedstraw. It is found in almost every hedge and also on disturbed and waste ground, in fens and on coastal shingle; it flowers May–June. Its small round fruits stick to clothing.

BORAGE FAMILY **1 Russian Comfrey**
Symphytum × uplandicum. This hybrid
fodder plant has become widely established
on roadsides; its flowers, which appear from
May–July, are usually bright blue or dull
purple. **2 Common Comfrey** *S. officinale* is
the commonest native British comfrey and is
found in marshes and by fresh water. It has
either creamy white or dull purple flowers
which appear from May–July. It is one of the
parents of Russian Comfrey.

BORAGE FAMILY **1 Houndstongue** *Cynoglossum officinale* has a strong mousy smell, soft downy leaves, small maroon flowers from June–August, and flattened spiny fruits which adhere to clothing and animal fur. It is widespread in bare, dry turf on chalk, limestone and sand. **2 Borage** *Borago officinalis* is a culinary herb which is often to be found on waste ground. Its distinctive bright blue flowers with their swept-back petals appear May–September.

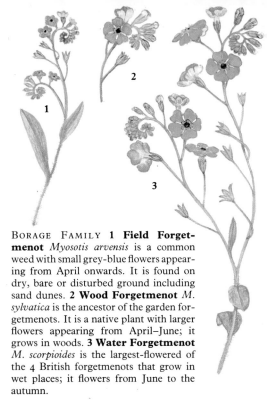

BORAGE FAMILY **1 Field Forgetmenot** *Myosotis arvensis* is a common weed with small grey-blue flowers appearing from April onwards. It is found on dry, bare or disturbed ground including sand dunes. **2 Wood Forgetmenot** *M. sylvatica* is the ancestor of the garden forgetmenots. It is a native plant with larger flowers appearing from April–June; it grows in woods. **3 Water Forgetmenot** *M. scorpioides* is the largest-flowered of the 4 British forgetmenots that grow in wet places; it flowers from June to the autumn.

BORAGE FAMILY **1 Viper's Bugloss**
Echium vulgare. A big stand of this
bugloss with its brilliant blue flowers is
one of the most gorgeous sights in the
British flora. It grows on dry, bare spots
on light soils, especially chalk, and flowers
June–September. **2 Green Alkanet**
Pentaglottis sempervirens is a garden plant
that is becoming widely established in
woods and hedge-banks. Its bright blue,
white-eyed flowers appear between late
April and August.

VERBENA FAMILY **1 Vervain** *Verbena officinalis* is the only native British representative of a great family widespread in the tropics. It has stiff square stems and spikes of small 2-lipped lilac flowers from June–October; often in dry, bare or sparsely grassy places, on limy soils. LABIATE FAMILY **2 Wood Sage** *Teucrium scorodonia* is the only common British labiate with pale yellow-green flowers. It grows in woods, scrubs and heaths, avoiding lime, and flowers July–September.

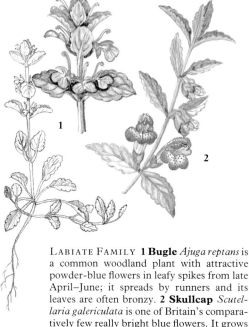

LABIATE FAMILY **1 Bugle** *Ajuga reptans* is a common woodland plant with attractive powder-blue flowers in leafy spikes from late April–June; it spreads by runners and its leaves are often bronzy. **2 Skullcap** *Scutellaria galericulata* is one of Britain's comparatively few really bright blue flowers. It grows in wet grassy places, often by rivers, streams and lakes, and flowers from June–September. It received its name because of the shape of the 2-lipped flowers after they have finished flowering.

LABIATE FAMILY **1 Self-heal** *Prunella vulgaris* has squarish heads of violet-purple flowers, which appear from June–November, and is very common in grassy places and in open woods; its name refers to its use as a cure-all in the Middle Ages. **2 Ground Ivy** *Glechoma hederacea* has a variety of names, including Ale-hoof, which refer to its former use in flavouring beer. It is very common in hedge-banks and bare places, creeping along the ground, and flowers from March–June.

LABIATE FAMILY **Black Horehound** *Ballota nigra* is a strong-smelling straggly plant of waysides and waste places with pink-purple flowers, 2-lipped like most labiates, which appear from June–September. Its curious name derives from another much less common labiate, White Horehound *Marrubium vulgare*, which is downy white all over and was once used as a cure for coughs. Hore means hoar or white, and hound is corrupted from an old word meaning plant.

143

LABIATE FAMILY The Dead-nettles *Lamium* are so called because their nettle-like leaves do not sting. **1 White Dead-nettle** *L. album*, also called White Archangel, is a common wayside weed which flowers from March–November, or even later in mild winters. **2 Red Dead-nettle** *L. purpureum* is a very common garden weed that flowers throughout the year, except in hard frosts. **3 Henbit Dead-nettle** *L. amplexicaule* has unstalked upper leaves and less conspicuous flowers than Red Dead-nettle; it is also a weed of cultivation and flowers from March–October.

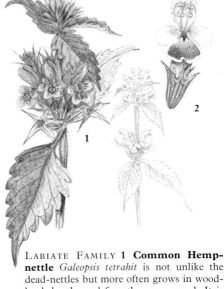

LABIATE FAMILY **1 Common Hemp-nettle** *Galeopsis tetrahit* is not unlike the dead-nettles but more often grows in woodland, heaths and fens than as a weed. It is taller than Red Dead-nettle and its stems are swollen at the leaf-junctions; flowering June–September. **2 Large-flowered Hemp-nettle** *G. speciosa* is larger still with pale yellow flowers with purple lower lips July–September. A weed of cultivation and bare places, it is more common in the north.

LABIATE FAMILY **Yellow Archangel**
Lamiastrum galeobdolon is common in woods
in late spring, May and June. Its butter-
coloured flowers are 2-lipped, like almost
all labiates (a few have no upper lip), and it
spreads by means of long creeping runners.
Nobody quite knows why this plant and the
White Dead-nettle (p. 144) share the name
Archangel. Perhaps some imaginative person
saw a resemblance to an archangel in the
flower, as another did to a frog in the Frog
Orchid.

LABIATE FAMILY **1 Hedge Woundwort**
Stachys sylvatica is one of the commonest
hedge-bank plants. It is strong-smelling, with
beetroot-red flowers – a rare colour in the
European flora – that appear from June–
October. **2 Marsh Woundwort** *S. palustris*,
as its name suggests, prefers marshy ground
and freshwater margins. It is a much less
aromatic plant, with much pinker flowers,
which appear from July–September. The
soft downy leaves of woundworts were used
to dress wounds in the Middle Ages.

LABIATE FAMILY **Betony** *Stachys officinalis* is a close relative of the two woundworts on p. 147, which grows in grassy and heathy places on slightly acid soils. Its shorter spikes of red-purple flowers, intermediate in colour between the two woundworts, appear from June–October. The name Betony derives, via the Roman author Pliny, from a Spanish tribe, the Vettones, and is also sometimes used for a quite unrelated plant, Water Figwort or Water Betony (p. 156).

LABIATE FAMILY Mints *Mentha* are highly aromatic plants with small lilac-purple flowers in heads or spikes that appear from July–October. **1 Spear Mint** *M. spicata* is the species grown in gardens and associated with roast lamb; it often escapes on to waste ground. **2 Water Mint** *M. aquatica* has rounded heads of flowers, grows in marshes and by fresh water. **3 Corn Mint** *M. arvensis* is similar but smaller, with no terminal head. It grows on bare damp ground and as a weed of cultivation. All 3 have distinct scents or savours.

LABIATE FAMILY **Gipsywort** *Lycopus europaeus* is like an unscented mint and is commonly found by streams, rivers, ponds and lakes and in marshy places. Its smaller white flowers, which appear from July–September, occur in heads at the base of the leaves up the stem. It is said to owe its name to gypsies using it to stain themselves brown with its juice; or, perhaps more likely, people who were not real gypsies used it to make themselves more gypsy-like.

LABIATE FAMILY **1 Marjoram** *Origanum vulgare* is one of the wild European plants which is still widely used as a herb. It is pleasantly aromatic and its pale purple flowers with dark purple bracts at the base appear from July–September in chalk and limestone grassland and scrub. **2 Wild Basil** *Clinopodium vulgare* grows in similar places and flowers at the same time; however, it is shorter, only faintly aromatic and lacks the dark purple bracts.

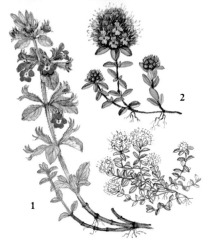

LABIATE FAMILY **1 Basil Thyme** *Acinos arvensis* is only slightly aromatic and has violet-purple flowers which appear from June–September. It grows in bare spots on chalk and limestone soils and must not be confused with the pinker-flowered Wild Basil (p. 151). **2 Wild Thyme** *Thymus praecox* is well known for its sweet smell and has pinkish-purple flowers like Marjoram (p. 151) and Wild Basil, not violet-purple like Basil Thyme, which appear from June–September. It is a low-growing plant and is common in short turf on both acid and limy soils, on heaths and downs throughout the British Isles.

NIGHTSHADE FAMILY **1 Bittersweet** or **Woody Nightshade** *Solanum dulcamara* is often confused with Deadly Nightshade (p. 154) although it is a quite distinct and less poisonous plant. It grows in a wide variety of bare and bushy habitats from coastal shingle to wood and scrub; it flowers from May–September and the berries are first green, then yellow and finally red. **2 Black Nightshade** *S. nigrum* has white flowers from July–October and is named after its black berries. It is a widespread weed but tends to avoid limy soils.

NIGHTSHADE FAMILY **Deadly Nightshade** *Atropa bella-donna* is aptly named as its black cherry-sized berries are among the most poisonous of any European plants. However, despite this, Italian ladies once used the juice of the berries to dilate the pupils of their eyes, hence its other name Belladonna. It grows in woods and scrub on chalk and limestone; the dull purple flowers appear from June–September and the berries a few weeks later.

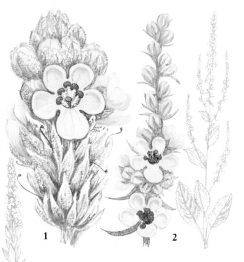

1

2

FIGWORT FAMILY **1 Great Mullein** or **Aaron's Rod** *Verbascum thapsus* is a tall plant, up to 2m high, with leaves and stems covered with thick white wool; the stamens of the bright yellow flowers also have white woolly hairs. It grows in dry grassy and bare places and flowers from June–August. **2 Dark Mullein** *V. nigrum* is a shorter plant without any white woolly hairs; it has purple hairs on the stamens of its smaller flowers and a strong preference for limy soils.

FIGWORT FAMILY **1 Common Figwort** *Scrophularia nodosa* is a tall, rather unpleasant-smelling plant of woods and scrub. Its stems are square and the small dull red-brown flowers, which appear from June–September, are especially attractive to wasps. **2 Water Figwort** or **Water Betony** *S. auriculata* is best distinguished by its winged stems and its white-edged sepals; it grows in marshes and by fresh water. Yellow Figwort *S. vernalis*, with yellow flowers which appear in spring, sometimes escapes from gardens onto waste ground.

FIGWORT FAMILY **1 Common Toadflax** *Linaria vulgaris* has greyish yellow leaves and 2-lipped flowers like small snapdragons June–October. It is common on waysides and in waste places. **2 Monkey Flower** *Mimulus guttatus* from North America is widely naturalised in marshes and by rivers and streams, especially in the north of England and Scotland. Its large, red-spotted, bright yellow, 2-lipped flowers appear June–September.

FIGWORT FAMILY **Foxglove** *Digitalis purpurea*. Foxes wearing gloves is the kind of grotesque fantasy to which the ancestors who named our flowers were prone! However, the Foxglove is one of the tallest, most handsome and conspicuous of British wild flowers and is found in woods and scrub, and on heaths, moors and mountains, especially on acid soils. The flowers appear from June–September. Foxglove is the source of the drug digitalis which is used in the treatment of human heart conditions (physical ones, not psychological ones!).

FIGWORT FAMILY **Red Bartsia** *Odontites verna* is commonly found on bare and disturbed ground. It is a semi-parasitic plant and lives on the roots of other species; its 2-lipped pink or purplish flowers appear from July–September. Yellow Bartsia *Parentucellia viscosa* is a yellow-flowered plant with sticky hairs; it grows on dunes and in damp sandy and grassy places in the south and west, mainly near the coast. Unlike that of Red Bartsia, the stem of Yellow Bartsia is usually unbranched.

FIGWORT FAMILY **1 Germander Speed-well** *Veronica chamaedrys* is the largest and most brightly coloured of the commoner British species of speedwell; its bright azure-blue flowers appear from mid-April to June in many grassy places. Its name refers to the likeness of its leaves to those of some species of germander (*Teucrium*). **2 Heath Speed-well** *V. officinalis* has smaller, more lilac-coloured flowers; it appears from May–August in dry grassy and heathy places and open woods.

FIGWORT FAMILY **1 Common Field Speedwell** *Veronica persica* is an extremely common arable weed with sky-blue flowers, with a white lower lip, that appear throughout the year except during the hardest frosts. Originally a native of Asia, it first appeared in Europe early in the 19th century and has since become one of the commonest and most widespread European weeds. **2 Ivy-leaved Speedwell** *V. hederifolia* is another common weed found in gardens and on bare ground. It has 2 forms – one with blue flowers, one with smaller lilac flowers – both of which appear from March–August.

1

2

FIGWORT FAMILY **1 Thyme-leaved Speedwell** *Veronica serpyllifolia* is a common plant in bare and sparsely grassy places, but much less of a garden weed than some other speedwells. Its pale blue, or sometimes white, flowers appear from April–October. On mountains an attractive form with larger flowers can be found. **2 Wall Speedwell** *V. arvensis* is another plant commonly found on bare ground, and also often growing on walls, that is hardly big or troublesome enough to be stigmatised as a weed. In very dry conditions it may be only a centimetre or two high. Its tiny blue flowers appear from April, or even March, to October. Both plants grow throughout the British Isles.

FIGWORT FAMILY **1 Brooklime** *Veronica beccabunga* is the commonest, most widespread and largest-flowered of the water speedwells; its bright blue flowers appear in all kinds of wet places, including wet cart ruts in woods, from May–September. **2 Blue Water Speedwell** *V. anagallis-aquatica* has narrower leaves and paler blue flowers which appear from June–August. **3 Pink Water Speedwell** *V. catenata* can be distinguished from Blue Water Speedwell by its pink flowers and often purplish stems. The last 2 species grow mainly by fresh water and in marshy spots and often hybridise. The hybrids are often taller than either of the 2 parent species.

FIGWORT FAMILY **Eyebright** *Euphrasia officinalis* is a very variable plant in height, branching and flower size and colour. Its flowers are usually white, often tinged with purple, sometimes with purple veins or a yellow spot; they appear from June–October. Eyebright is semi-parasitic on the roots of other plants, and grows in a wide variety of open habitats – grassland (both calcareous and acid), sand dunes, downs, heaths, moors and mountains. Its name derives from its former use as an aid to clear the sight.

1

2

FIGWORT FAMILY **1 Yellow Rattle** *Rhinanthus minor* gets its name from the way its dried seeds rattle inside the inflated fruiting head when ripe. It grows in grassy and heathy places and on moors and mountains, producing yellow flowers with open mouths from May–September. **2 Common Cow-wheat** *Melampyrum pratense* grows in similar but often shadier places than Yellow Rattle but can be distinguished by its flowers which grow in pairs up the stem and have closed not open mouths. Both species are semi-parasitic on the roots of other plants.

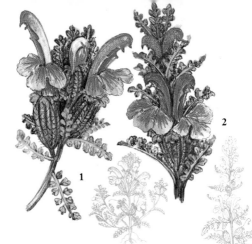

FIGWORT FAMILY **Lousewort** *Pedicularis sylvatica* is a fairly common rather low-growing plant found on moors, damp heathland and bogs; it has unbranched stems and flowers from April–July. **2 Marsh Louse-wort** *P. palustris* is a taller plant with a branched stem and flowers of a rather sharper, redder pink from May–September. It grows in wetter places in marshes and on damp heaths; it is also known as Red Rattle for the same reason as Yellow Rattle (p. 165).

BROOMRAPE FAMILY **Common Broomrape** *Orobranche minor* neither needs nor has any green colouring as it obtains its nourishment by parasitising the roots of other plants; it gets its name from a large but now uncommon species that thus 'rapes' Broom. Common Broomrape may be purplish, reddish or yellowish and parasitises pea-flowers or composites; it flowers June–September in grassy places. Ivy Broomrape *O. hederae* is similar but always on ivy.

BUTTERWORT FAMILY **Common Butterwort**
Pinguicula vulgaris is one of the small number of
British and European insectivorous plants. Its leaves
are arranged in a basal rosette and have edges which
roll inwards to entrap and subsequently digest insects unwary enough to settle on them. The violet-
like flowers, with a white throat patch, appear singly
on leafless stems from May–July. Common Butterwort grows only in bogs and fens and on wet
heaths and moors, mainly in the north and west of
Britain. A smaller and more local western species,
Pale Butterwort *P. lusitanica*, has lighter-coloured
flowers with a yellow throat.

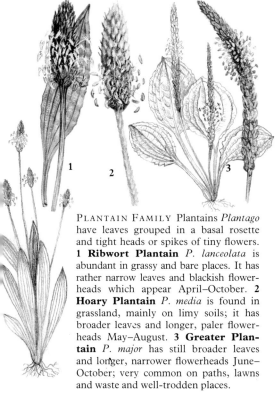

PLANTAIN FAMILY Plantains *Plantago* have leaves grouped in a basal rosette and tight heads or spikes of tiny flowers. **1 Ribwort Plantain** *P. lanceolata* is abundant in grassy and bare places. It has rather narrow leaves and blackish flower-heads which appear April–October. **2 Hoary Plantain** *P. media* is found in grassland, mainly on limy soils; it has broader leaves and longer, paler flowerheads May–August. **3 Greater Plantain** *P. major* has still broader leaves and longer, narrower flowerheads June–October; very common on paths, lawns and waste and well-trodden places.

169

PLANTAIN FAMILY **1 Buckshorn Plantain** *Plantago coronopus* is the only native British plantain to have pinnate or pinnately-lobed leaves. The flowerheads are like the Greater Plantain's (p. 169) but much shorter, with yellow stamens. It grows in dry, bare and often sandy places, most frequently on the coast, and flowers from May–October. **2 Sea Plantain** *P. maritima* has much longer flowerheads and long narrow veined leaves, flowers from June–September and grows in saltmarshes.

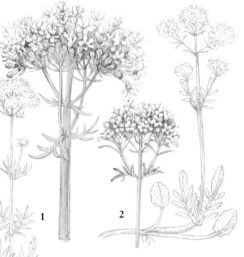

VALERIAN FAMILY **1 Common Valerian**
Valeriana officinalis is a tall plant with pinnate
leaves and conspicuous clusters of small pink
flowers that appear from June–August; it
grows in both damp and dry woods and grassland. Its root used to be regarded as a cure
for hysteria and other nervous conditions.
2 Marsh Valerian *V. dioica* is smaller and
earlier flowering (May–June), with characteristic oval root leaves. It grows only in fens
and marshes.

VALERIAN FAMILY **Red Valerian** or
Spur Valerian *Centranthus ruber* is conspicuous on cliffs, rocks, walls, railway cut-
tings and steep banks from May–September.
Its flowers are usually deep reddish-pink, but
a white form is not uncommon. A native of the
Mediterranean region and Portugal, it long
ago escaped from gardens and established itself in the wild in many parts of southern and
eastern England, also near the coast in SE
Scotland and eastern Ireland.

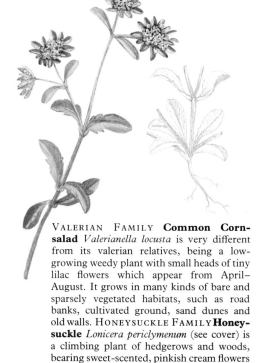

VALERIAN FAMILY **Common Corn-salad** *Valerianella locusta* is very different from its valerian relatives, being a low-growing weedy plant with small heads of tiny lilac flowers which appear from April–August. It grows in many kinds of bare and sparsely vegetated habitats, such as road banks, cultivated ground, sand dunes and old walls. HONEYSUCKLE FAMILY **Honey-suckle** *Lonicera periclymenum* (see cover) is a climbing plant of hedgerows and woods, bearing sweet-scented, pinkish cream flowers June–October. Its fruit is a red berry.

173

TEASEL FAMILY **1 Small Scabious**
Scabiosa columbaria grows in chalk and
limestone grassland. Its tiny flowers are
packed into a conspicuous head mixed
with dark bristles and appear from June–
October. **2 Field Scabious** *Knautia
arvensis* is a stouter taller plant with
broader leaves and larger flowerheads
with no dark bristles. It flowers from
June-October and is common in dry
grassy places, less so in cornfields.

TEASEL FAMILY **1 Devilsbit Scabious** *Succisa pratensis* has untoothed leaves and smaller darker flowerheads than the 2 opposite. It is common in damp grassy and heathy places, much less so in chalk grassland, and flowers June–October. BELLFLOWER FAMILY **2 Sheep's Scabious** *Jasione montana* is shorter than the other scabiouses, with untoothed, often wavy-edged leaves, and bluer flowers appearing May–September in dry grassland away from limy soils.

TEASEL FAMILY **Teasel** *Dipsacus fullonum*.
This common plant of waysides and waste
ground has tall prickly stems, numerous
prickles and white pimples on its leaves and,
from July–August, tiny lilac-purple flowers
which nestle in a stout prickly conical head;
the dead stems and flowerheads persist
through the winter. Fuller's Teasel is a cultivated form; its fruiting heads with hooked
bracts were once used in weaving to raise the
nap.

BELLFLOWER FAMILY **1 Harebell** *Campanula rotundifolia*, known as Bluebell in Scotland, is a very common plant of dry grassland and heaths, on both acid and limy soils. Its gay bell-shaped flowers appear from July–October. **2 Clustered Bellflower** *C. glomerata* is one of the most gorgeous British and European wildflowers. It grows most often on chalk or limestone downs and its rich purple flowers appear from June–October.

BELLFLOWER FAMILY **Nettle-leaved Bellflower** *Campanula trachelium* is a tall handsome plant which is found in woods, scrub and hedge-banks, usually on limy soils, in southern England and the Midlands. Its violet-blue flowers with short triangular petal-lobes appear from July–September; the upper flowers open before the lower ones. Unlike the Giant Bellflower (opposite) its stems are rather sharply angled.

BELLFLOWER FAMILY **Giant Bell-flower** *Campanula latifolia* is a taller plant than Nettle-leaved Bellflower (opposite) with bluntly-angled stems and larger paler flowers with longer narrower petal-lobes; it flowers from July–September and the lower flowers open first. It grows in woods, scrub and hedgebanks mainly in hill districts and most commonly in the north of England; south of the Thames it is quite rare.

COMPOSITE FAMILY **Hemp Agrimony**
Eupatorium cannabinum. The great Composite or Daisy Family is characterised by
tiny flowers collected into heads which look
like whole flowers. These florets are of 2
kinds, with and without a strap-like ray; a
typical daisy-like composite has disc florets in
the middle, ringed by ray florets. Hemp Agrimony, which is found in damp places such as
woods marshes and fens, has disc florets only;
it flowers from July–September.

COMPOSITE FAMILY **1 Goldenrod** *Solidago virgaurea* has bright yellow flowers with short rays which appear from June–September; it is found in woods, scrub, heathland and grassy places and prefers acid soils. **2 Canadian Goldenrod** *S. canadensis* is a much taller garden escape from North America that is established widely on roadsides and waste ground and by streams. Its smaller flowers, in larger and more conspicuous spikes, appear July–September.

COMPOSITE FAMILY **1 Daisy** *Bellis perennis* is the common and attractive denizen of lawns so disliked by tidy gardeners. It flowers throughout the year except in prolonged hard frosts. **2 Scentless Mayweed** *Matricaria perforata* is a common weed of bare and disturbed ground, with large daisy-like flowers appearing from April–October. **3 Sea Mayweed** *M. maritima* is a stouter, fleshier relative found on shingle and bare ground by the sea. **4 Scented Mayweed** *Chamomilla recutita* has smaller flowers than Scented Mayweed and is slightly aromatic; it grows in similar places and flowers from May–September.

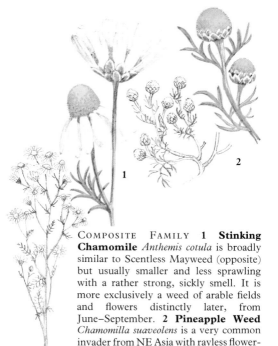

COMPOSITE FAMILY **1 Stinking Chamomile** *Anthemis cotula* is broadly similar to Scentless Mayweed (opposite) but usually smaller and less sprawling with a rather strong, sickly smell. It is more exclusively a weed of arable fields and flowers distinctly later, from June–September. **2 Pineapple Weed** *Chamomilla suaveolens* is a very common invader from NE Asia with rayless flower-heads appearing from May–November. It is widespread in bare and waste places, especially well-trodden ones, such as farm-yards and gateways.

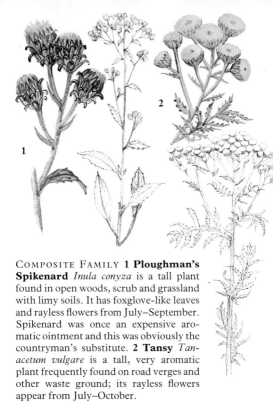

COMPOSITE FAMILY **1 Ploughman's Spikenard** *Inula conyza* is a tall plant found in open woods, scrub and grassland with limy soils. It has foxglove-like leaves and rayless flowers from July–September. Spikenard was once an expensive aromatic ointment and this was obviously the countryman's substitute. **2 Tansy** *Tanacetum vulgare* is a tall, very aromatic plant frequently found on road verges and other waste ground; its rayless flowers appear from July–October.

COMPOSITE FAMILY **1 Sea Aster**
Aster tripolium has 2 forms, one with
and one without pale purple ray florets.
Both forms flower from July–October
and grow commonly in saltmarshes all
round the coast. **2 Michaelmas Daisy**
A. novi-belgii is a garden escape from
North America, now increasingly common in roadsides and other waste places
and in marshes or by streams. Its daisy-
like flowers with white or purple ray florets appear August–November.

COMPOSITE FAMILY **Mountain Everlasting** *Antennaria dioica* is a low creeping plant with rooting runners; the undersides of the leaves are covered with short white wool. Its white or pink rayless flowers appear in June–July; the stamens and styles, denoting male or female, are on different plants. It grows on heaths and moors and in mountain grassland, commonly in the Scottish Highlands and much less so in other parts of the north and west.

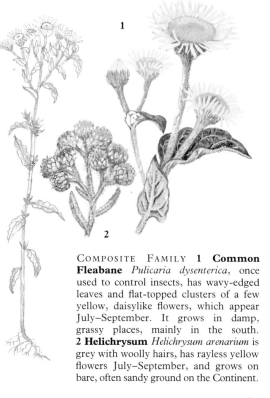

COMPOSITE FAMILY **1 Common Fleabane** *Pulicaria dysenterica*, once used to control insects, has wavy-edged leaves and flat-topped clusters of a few yellow, daisylike flowers, which appear July–September. It grows in damp, grassy places, mainly in the south. **2 Helichrysum** *Helichrysum arenarium* is grey with woolly hairs, has rayless yellow flowers July–September, and grows on bare, often sandy ground on the Continent.

COMPOSITE FAMILY **Butterbur** *Petasites hybridus* forms large patches in damp places such as road verges and streamsides, where its huge rhubarb-like leaves, up to 1m across, are conspicuous in summer. The brush-like heads of rayless flowers appear in early spring (March–May) before the leaves, in 2 forms. In male plants the florets almost all have stamens only, in female plants styles; in Britain, female plants are found only in the north of England.

COMPOSITE FAMILY **1 Yarrow** *Achillea millefolium* is a very common, very aromatic plant of grassland with feathery pinnate leaves which often betray its presence in lawns. Its small rayed flowerheads are usually white but may be pink and appear from June–November. **2 Sneezewort** *A. ptarmica* has narrow undivided leaves and looser clusters of always white flowers from July–September; it grows in damp heathy or grassy places on neutral or acid soils.

COMPOSITE FAMILY **Mugwort** *Artemisia vulgaris*. This very common, slightly aromatic plant of waste ground owes its name to having once been used to keep away midges. Its leaves are silvery beneath, and its small rayless flowerheads appear from July–September. Wormwood *A. absinthium* is a much more aromatic plant with leaves which are silvery on both sides and larger, yellower flowerheads which do not appear till August. It was formerly used in the distilling of absinth.

1

2

COMPOSITE FAMILY **Bur Marigold** *Bidens* has rayless flowers which appear from late July–October and flattened fruits that cling to human clothing and animal fur by means of 2 hooked bristles. It grows in damp places by fresh water. **1 Trifid Bur Marigold** *B. tripartita* has erect flowerheads and leaves which usually have 2 lobes at the base. **2 Nodding Bur Marigold** *B. cernua* has larger nodding flowerheads and leaves usually without lobes. Both are commonest in southern England and the Midlands.

COMPOSITE FAMILY **Ox-eye Daisy**
Leucanthemum vulgare is one of the commonest grassland plants, usually when there is some lime in the soil; its large flowerheads appear May–September. It is so named because, rather surprisingly, it reminded the ancient Greeks of the eyes of their oxen. The much larger Shasta Daisy *L. maximum* is a garden escape and flowers from July–September.

COMPOSITE FAMILY **Corn Marigold** *Chrysanthemum segetum* now rarely turns cornfields completely yellow, thanks to modern herbicides, but it is still not uncommon on the borders of fields or waste ground. Its bright yellow daisy-like flowers appear from June–October; its stems are slightly greyish green. The marigold most often seen in gardens and on waste ground is *Calendula officinalis* with similar but bright orange flowers.

COMPOSITE FAMILY **Coltsfoot** *Tussilago farfara* is the classic early spring wild flower. Its narrowly-rayed flowerheads appear long before the leaves, as early as late January in mild winters, and are mostly over by the end of April; the large leaves, which reminded our ancestors of a colt's foot, surface in April or May on numerous kinds of often clayey bare ground. The fruits make a dandelion-like clock. In the medieval pharmacopoeia Coltsfoot had some repute as a cough cure.

1

2

COMPOSITE FAMILY **1 Ragwort** *Senecio jacobaea* is a common weed of dry pastures that have been overgrazed, especially by rabbits, which do not eat it. It is almost hairless and its flowers appear June–November. It is a favourite food-plant of the black-and-yellow striped caterpillars of the red and black cinnabar moth. **2 Hoary Ragwort** *S. erucifolius* flowers a month later in similar grassy places; it is grey, downy and has more narrowly-lobed leaves.

COMPOSITE FAMILY **1 Oxford Ragwort**
Senecio squalidus, a native of Sicily, escaped
from the Oxford Botanic Garden from where
its seeds were wafted along the railways by the
draught of trains until it is now very common
and widespread on waste ground in England
and Wales; it flowers from April–November.
2 Marsh Ragwort *S. aquaticus* is more
sprawling than Ragwort (p. 195) and grows
only in wet meadows and marshes; its flowerheads appear from June–September.

COMPOSITE FAMILY **1 Groundsel** *Senecio vulgaris* is an abundant and universal weed of bare ground; its usually rayless flowers appear throughout the year except in the hardest winters. **2 Heath Groundsel** *S. sylvaticus* is larger and appears from July–October in dry sandy and heathy places; it smells foetid and is greyish with sticky hairs. **3 Sticky Groundsel** *S. viscosus* flowers from May–October on bare and waste ground; it is even more foetid and conspicuously sticky. The tips of the sepal-like bracts of Groundsel are black, of Heath Groundsel green, and of Sticky Groundsel purplish.

COMPOSITE FAMILY **Carline Thistle**
Carlina vulgaris is fairly common in chalk
and limestone grassland and on sand
dunes, but in Scotland is almost confined
to the coast. Its thistle-like leaves are
both prickly and cottony and its rayless
flowerheads have ray-like yellow bracts
which fold up in wet weather; it flowers
from July–September. It owes its name to
the medieval Emperor Charlemagne who
used the continental species *C. acaulis* to
cure disease among his soldiers.

COMPOSITE FAMILY **Lesser Burdock**
Arctium minus has large, broadly heart-shaped leaves and rayless purple flower-heads which appear from July–September in woods and other shady or waste places. The dead stems last through the winter and the dried fruiting heads or burs adhere tenaciously to human clothing and animal fur. Greater Burdock *A. lappa* has larger flowerheads but is rather hard for non-botanists to distinguish from Lesser Burdock.

COMPOSITE FAMILY **1 Creeping Thistle** *Cirsium arvense* is one of the most widespread and pestilential weeds in Britain, being perennial and hard to eradicate. It forms patches in grassy and waste places and has smallish lilac-purple flowers from June–September. **2 Spear Thistle** *C. vulgare*, found in similar habitats, is much taller, to 3m, and has extremely sharp spines on its leaves; its large purple flowers appear July–September.

COMPOSITE FAMILY **1 Marsh Thistle**
Cirsium palustre is a tall plant, up to 3m
high, found in mainly damp grassy places
and fens. Its smallish purple (occasionally
white) flowerheads have stalks covered
in spines and appear June–September.
2 Welted Thistle *Cardus acanthoides* has
stalks on its flowerheads which are spine-
less at the top; it also flowers earlier, from
the end of May, and grows in drier grassy
places, often on hedge-banks.

COMPOSITE FAMILY **1 Dwarf Thistle** *Cirsium acaule* is the most distinctive British thistle, for its large purple flower-heads, usually without a stalk, nestle in a rosette of prickly leaves. It flowers from late June–September and grows only in grassland on limy soils. **2 Musk Thistle** *Cardus nutans* is another lime lover; its rather reddish-purple nodding flower-heads appear late May–September.

COMPOSITE FAMILY **1 Black Knap-weed** *Centaurea nigra*, originally Knob-weed, is often called Hardhead because of its hard knob-like buds. It may or may not have apparent rays with forked tips but always has undivided leaves. **2 Greater Knapweed** *C. scabiosa* has larger, always rayed flowers and pinnate leaves. Both grow in grassland and flower from June–September but Greater Knapweed prefers limy soils.

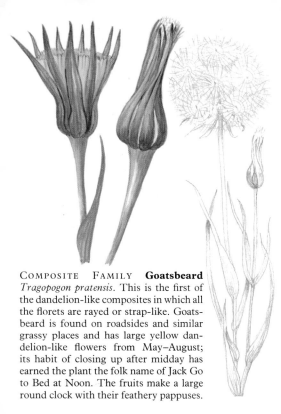

COMPOSITE FAMILY **Goatsbeard**
Tragopogon pratensis. This is the first of
the dandelion-like composites in which all
the florets are rayed or strap-like. Goatsbeard is found on roadsides and similar
grassy places and has large yellow dandelion-like flowers from May–August;
its habit of closing up after midday has
earned the plant the folk name of Jack Go
to Bed at Noon. The fruits make a large
round clock with their feathery pappuses.

COMPOSITE FAMILY **1 Cornflower** *Centaurea cyanus* bears bright blue flowers June–August on waste ground, but no longer in cornfields because of modern herbicides. **2 Chicory** or **Succory** *Cichorium intybus*, our only blue-flowered dandelion-like plant, appears June–September in waste places and on roadsides on limy soils. Its blanched leaves make a salad, and its roots, dried, roasted and ground, are used as an additive to coffee.

COMPOSITE FAMILY **1 Smooth Sow-thistle** *Sonchus oleraceus* is an abundant weed of bare and waste places. It has milky juice, softly spiny leaves clasping the stem with arrow-shaped points, and pale yellow flower-heads from May–November. **2 Prickly Sow-thistle** *S. asper* is very similar but has slightly sharper spines and the leaves clasping the stem have rounded lobes. **3 Perennial Sow-thistle** *S. arvensis* is a much taller weed, with large deep yellow flowerheads from July–September and sticky yellow hairs on the sepal-like bracts.

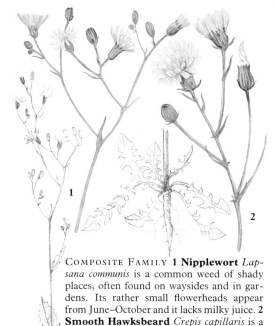

COMPOSITE FAMILY **1 Nipplewort** *Lapsana communis* is a common weed of shady places, often found on waysides and in gardens. Its rather small flowerheads appear from June–October and it lacks milky juice. **2 Smooth Hawksbeard** *Crepis capillaris* is a very common plant of grassy and waste places and is sometimes found on lawns. Its upper leaves clasp the stem with arrow-shaped points; the flowerheads, with the outer sepal-like bracts recurved, appear from June–November.

COMPOSITE FAMILY **1 Mouse-ear Hawkweed** *Pilosella officinarum* is a low-growing plant with creeping runners, shaggy leaves with white hairs and solitary lemon-yellow flowerheads which appear from May–October. **2 Dandelion** *Taraxacum officinale* is the all too common weed of lawns and waste places. Its solitary flowerheads on hollow leafless stems appear March–November and throughout mild winters. The name derives from *dent de lion* (French for lion's tooth) which refers to the shape of its leaves.

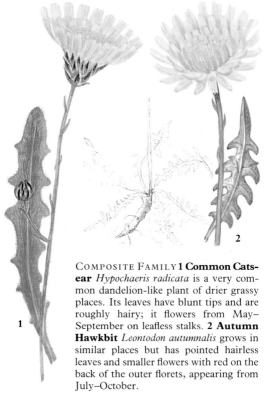

COMPOSITE FAMILY **1 Common Cats-ear** *Hypochaeris radicata* is a very common dandelion-like plant of drier grassy places. Its leaves have blunt tips and are roughly hairy; it flowers from May–September on leafless stalks. **2 Autumn Hawkbit** *Leontodon autumnalis* grows in similar places but has pointed hairless leaves and smaller flowers with red on the back of the outer florets, appearing from July–October.

COMPOSITE FAMILY **1 Rough Hawkbit**
Leontodon hispidus is a common dandelion-
like plant very characteristic of limy grass-
lands. It is shaggily hairy and its flowerheads
on leafless stalks appear from June–October.
2 Lesser Hawkbit *L. taraxacoides* is smaller,
more low-growing and much less hairy; the
outer florets are grey-violet on the back and
appear from June–October. It grows in dry
grassy places and on sand dunes. In both
species the fruiting pappuses form a clock.

COMPOSITE FAMILY **1 Beaked Hawks-beard** *Crepis vesicaria* is a medium-tall plant found in drier grassy and waste places, and on walls. It has pinnate leaves and is orange-red on the back of the outer florets, appearing May–July. **2 Common Hawkweed** *Hieracium murorum* is a very variable plant common in all kinds of grassy and rather bare places such as walls, rocks and mountains. It may have few or many leaves or flowerheads and appears from June–November.

COMPOSITE FAMILY **1 Hawkweed Oxtongue** *Picris hieracioides* is very similar to some forms of Common Hawkweed (p. 211) but differs in its wavy-edged leaves and liking for limy grassland; it flowers July–October. **2 Bristly Oxtongue** *P. echioides* has wavy-edged leaves covered with whitish pimples and pale yellow flowerheads with broadly triangular sepal-like bracts; it flowers June–November in grassy places, especially on clay soils.

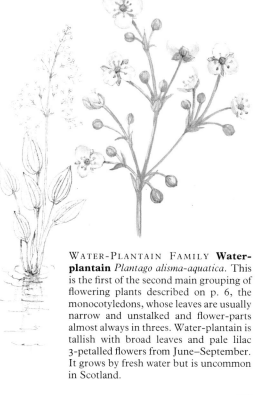

WATER-PLANTAIN FAMILY **Water-plantain** *Plantago alisma-aquatica*. This is the first of the second main grouping of flowering plants described on p. 6, the monocotyledons, whose leaves are usually narrow and unstalked and flower-parts almost always in threes. Water-plantain is tallish with broad leaves and pale lilac 3-petalled flowers from June–September. It grows by fresh water but is uncommon in Scotland.

WATER-PLANTAIN FAMILY **Arrowhead** *Sagittaria sagittifolia* is a striking tall waterside plant named after its large arrow-shaped aerial leaves; it also has oval or lanceolate floating leaves and narrow ribbon-shaped submerged ones. The handsome 3-petalled flowers, white with a purple spot at the base, appear in July–August. It grows in or by fairly shallow, still or flowing fresh water, including streams, rivers and ponds.

FLOWERING RUSH FAMILY **Flowering Rush** *Butomus umbellatus* is an even more strikingly handsome waterside plant than Arrowhead (opposite) that grows in and by all kinds of shallow fresh water. It is not related to the true rushes and has much broader, though still narrow, 3-cornered leaves than any rush. Its head of bright pink 6-petalled flowers appears in July–August and is followed by egg-shaped fruits which turn purple when they are ripe.

215

LILY FAMILY **1 Bog Asphodel** *Narthecium ossifragum* is easily identified at all stages by its small, distinctive, sword-shaped, iris-like leaves; spikes of starlike 6-petalled orange-yellow flowers appearing July–August; and deep orange fruits. It is widespread in bogs and wet heaths. **2 Solomon's Seal** *Polygonatum multiflorum*, very like the garden plant, flowers May–June in woods and scrub, mainly in the south. Its fruit is a blue–black berry.

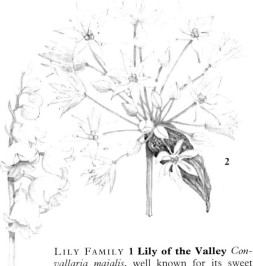

LILY FAMILY **1 Lily of the Valley** *Convallaria majalis*, well known for its sweet scent in gardens, grows wild in woods on limy soils in many parts of Britain. Its creamy-white, bell-shaped flowers appear in May–June. Its fruit is a red berry. **2 Ramsons** *Allium ursinum* is our commonest garlic, its leaves differing from those of Lily of the Valley by their strong, garlicky smell and brighter green colour. Its heads of star-shaped white flowers appear April–June in woods and on shady hedge-banks.

217

1

2

LILY FAMILY **1 Spring Squill** *Scilla verna* is a smaller plant than Bluebell with narrower curly leaves. It flowers from April–June on grassy cliff tops from south Devon up the west coast and down to Northumberland. **2 Bluebell** *Endymion non-scriptus* is better known as Wild Hyacinth in Scotland where the name Bluebell refers to the Harebell (p. 177). A Bluebell wood in full flower in May is one of the glories of the British countryside.

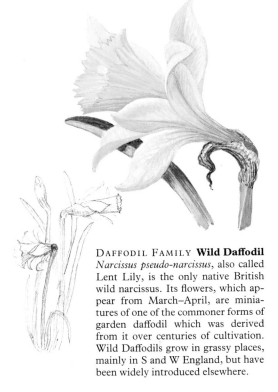

DAFFODIL FAMILY **Wild Daffodil**
Narcissus pseudo-narcissus, also called
Lent Lily, is the only native British
wild narcissus. Its flowers, which appear from March–April, are minia-
tures of one of the commoner forms of
garden daffodil which was derived
from it over centuries of cultivation.
Wild Daffodils grow in grassy places,
mainly in S and W England, but have
been widely introduced elsewhere.

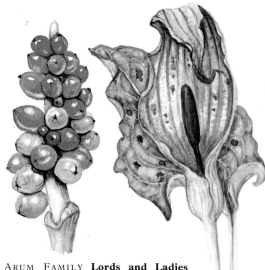

ARUM FAMILY **Lords and Ladies**
Arum maculatum has more folk names
than any other British plant; this one refers to the black spots on many of its leaves
recalling the days when the rich wore
black beauty spots to cover pimples.
Cuckoo-pint, another common name, has
unmentionable origins, quite uncon-
nected with the flowers appearing with the
cuckoo in April and May. It is found in
woods and on shady hedge-banks.

Iris Family **Yellow Iris** or **Yellow Flag** *Iris pseudacorus* is widespread and common in marshes and by fresh water. Its bright yellow flowers appear June–August; its leaves can be identified from those of other tall waterside plants by their raised midrib. The only other native British iris is Stinking Iris *I. foetidissima* which grows in drier places on cliffs and hedge-banks; it has dull purple flowers and leaves with an unpleasant smell when crushed.

ORCID FAMILY **White Helleborine**
Cephalanthera damasonium. There are many
more wild orchids in Britain than most people
realise and some of them are quite common.
White Helleborine is a speciality of the beechwoods of southern England and appears from
June–July. It has earned the name of
Poached-egg Plant from the yellow spot at
the base of the, usually hidden, lip of the
flower. Red Helleborine *C. rubra*, however, is
a great rarity with only a single remaining
secret locality in the Cotswolds.

ORCHID FAMILY **1 Bee Orchid** *Ophrys apifera* is so named because the lower lip of its flower has evolved to appear like the rear of a small bumblebee seeking nectar; this encourages real bees to do the same. It flowers in June–July in grassy places on chalk and limestone and on coastal dunes. **2 Fly Orchid** *O. insectifera* bears the same visual resemblance to and relationship with a small wasp; it appears in woods, scrub, fens and grassland on limy soils in May–June. Neither species is found in Scotland.

ORCHID FAMILY **1 Green-winged Orchid** *Orchis morio* has unspotted leaves and flowers varying from purple through pink to white, with green veins on the sepals hooded over the top. It flowers in May–June in grassland and open scrub and has suffered from the ploughing up of meadows. **2 Early Purple Orchid** *O. mascula* is one of the commonest and earliest flowering (April–June) British orchids; it grows in woods, scrub and grassland, usually on limy soils.

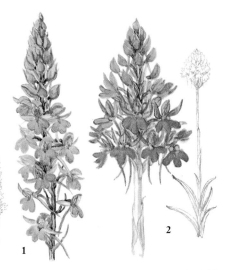

ORCHID FAMILY **1 Fragrant Orchid** *Gymnadenia conopsea* has an elongated spike of long-spurred pinkish-purple flowers, usually sweetly scented. **2 Pyramidal Orchid** *Anacamptis pyramidalis* has a much flatter, more pyramidal spike of rather hard pink, long-spurred flowers which may smell foxy. Both species grow in chalk and limestone grassland and scrub; the Fragrant also in fens, the Pyramidal on dunes. Both flower June–July.

ORCHID FAMILY **1 Early Marsh Orchid**
Dactylorhiza incarnata has flowers which
vary from white and yellow through pink to
purple and brick red; the sides of the lip fold
backwards. It flowers May–July. **2 Northern
Marsh Orchid** *D. purpurella* has wine-
purple flowers. **3 Southern Marsh Orchid**
D. praetermissa usually has rosy-purple flowers with unfolded sides from June–July. All 3
grow in marshy land, the latter 2 north and
south of a line from the Humber to S. Wales.

ORCHID FAMILY **1 Common Spotted Orchid** *Dactylorhiza fuchsii* is one of the commonest British orchids growing in grassland and scrub on chalk and limestone. Its pale pink, pale purple or white flowers have a conspicuous large tooth in the middle of the lip. **2 Heath Spotted Orchid** *D. maculata* is equally common but on acid soils in heaths, moors and bogs; its similar flowers have only an obscure central tooth. Both orchids appear June–August.

ORCHID FAMILY **1 Birdsnest Orchid**
Neottia nidus-avis is a honey-coloured plant
with no green colouring matter, being a sap-
rophyte which feeds on rotting vegetation
with the aid of a fungus partner. It flowers
from May–July in shady woods, especially
beechwoods. **2 Common Twayblade** *Lis-
tera ovata* is the least spectacular British
orchid, with unshowy yellow-green flowers
appearing in woods, scrub and grassland
from May–July. Its name derives from its 2
broad basal leaves.

1

2

ORCHID FAMILY **1 Greater Butterfly Orchid** *Platanthera chlorantha* has a single large pair of basal leaves, like the Common Twayblade (opposite), and a spike of long-spurred vanilla-scented white flowers. **2 Lesser Butterfly Orchid** *P. bifolia* is differentiated by slightly narrower leaves and by the fact that the pollen-masses in the middle of the flower are parallel, not diverging. Both appear in June–July in woods, open scrub and grassland; the Lesser also grows on moors and marshes.

Index of English Names

231

Index of Scientific Names

237